BARRON'S

NEW JERSEY GRADE 3

ELA/LITERACY TEST

Donna Mullaney, M.A.Ed.

About the Author

Donna Mullaney is currently Supervisor of English Language Arts, K–5, in Plainfield, New Jersey. She helped to create a curriculum in her district that aligned to the Common Core State Standards and has facilitated workshops on standards-based instruction and PARCC. Additionally, she worked as a literacy coach for the NJDOE, where she presented literacy workshops throughout the state, coached teachers, and supported best practices in literacy. After leaving the NJDOE, she continued to work as a literacy coach in Plainfield. Donna served as an interventionist for her district before becoming a supervisor. She began her career in Philadelphia, where she taught both primary and upper elementary grades. She is passionate about literacy and considers herself a lifelong learner. She currently resides in East Brunswick with her husband, Robert, and her Jack Russell Terrier, Penny. Her two daughters, Taryn and Kelly, also share her love of literature!

Acknowledgments

To my husband, Robert, thank you for your endless encouragement and support. To my daughters, Taryn and Kelly, your accomplishments are an inspiration to me. I am so proud of you both! To my mother, Joan, and father, Joseph, who instilled in me a good work ethic and the tenacity to tackle lofty goals. To my lifelong best friend, Marie, who helped to keep me sane through this process. A special thanks to my coworker and friend Joan, who serves as my sounding board for everything dealing with literacy and makes my job a place I enjoy working. Finally, to Stephenie, who encouraged me and nudged me every step of the way. We did it!

All inquiries should be addressed to:
Barron's Educational Series, Inc.
250 Wireless Boulevard
Hauppauge, NY 11788
www.barronseduc.com

ISBN: 978-1-4380-0735-9

Library of Congress Control Number: 2015944261

Date of Manufacture: August 2015
Manufactured by: B11R11

Printed in the United States of America
9 8 7 6 5 4 3 2 1

10% POST-CONSUMER WASTE
Paper contains a minimum of 10% post-consumer waste (PCW). Paper used in this book was derived from certified, sustainable forestlands.

Contents

Introduction

> **IMPORTANT NOTE:** Barron's has made every effort to ensure the content of this book is accurate as of press time, but the PARCC Assessments are constantly changing. Be sure to consult *www.parcconline.org* for all the latest testing information. Regardless of the changes that may be announced after press time, this book will still provide a strong framework for third-grade students preparing for the assessment.

Overview for Parents and Teachers

Third grade is an important year for students. The skills acquired in the previous grades have served as a foundation for the work required in this grade. Students in third grade will be required to apply critical thinking skills to what they read and write. The PARCC (Partnership for Assessment of Readiness for College and Careers) should not be looked at as just another test. It serves as an important tool to see how well a student is progressing.

The material covered on the third-grade PARCC assessment is designed to measure proficiency on the Common Core State Standards. These standards were developed to provide a consistent, clear understanding of what students are expected to learn at each grade level. They provide guidelines that help teachers and parents prepare students for college and careers.

In English Language Arts, there are three important changes, or shifts. The first change requires students to read an equal balance of literature and informational text. The second change requires students to read more challenging (complex) texts; when asked questions about what they have read, they will need to provide evidence from the text. "Text-based evidence" is a term you will frequently hear teachers referring to during reading and writing instruction. The third big change is an increased emphasis on building strong vocabulary. Developing a good understanding of vocabulary will help students to read and comprehend complex text. In writing, the standards in the third grade will require students to become proficient in writing opinion, informative/explanatory, and narrative writing pieces.

The standards in each section outline concepts that students in Grade Three should be able to do in each area.

- Reading Literature (10 standards)
- Reading Informational Text (10 standards)
- Foundation (4 standards—K–5 only)
- Writing (10 standards)
- Language (6 standards)
- Speaking and Listening (6 standards)

The mastery of each standard is the goal, since each standard increases in complexity through the grades. Students will be assessed on their understanding of grade-specific standards in reading and writing. For detailed information on the standards visit *http://www.corestandards.org/*.

This book was written to help New Jersey third-grade students achieve proficiency on the English Language Arts portion of the PARCC assessment. In addition to a complete practice test, it includes instructional study units in the following four skill areas:

1. Understanding test-taking strategies for Evidence-Based Selected-Response (EBSR) and Technology-Enhanced Constructed-Response (TECR) questions.
2. Reading literature and writing a narrative response.
3. Reading literature and writing a literary analysis.
4. Reading informational texts and writing in response to a research task.

Student achievement is greatly improved when the student, teacher, and parent or guardian work together. The practice exercises in this review book will enhance student performance on the assessment; however, no single resource could ever replace the cumulative learning experiences that have helped shape your child.

Please check with your child's teacher to see if there are any special instructions for testing procedures and if there are additional resources that may be helpful. Be sure your child has a good night's sleep before the assessment and a healthy breakfast on the morning of the test. If your child appears nervous, explain that most people experience some degree of test anxiety. Try to be reassuring and positive to help ease any anxiety.

Introduction for Students

Have you heard the news about the state test you will be taking in third grade? Third grade is very important because students in third grade will take the PARCC. Sure, students in other grades will also take it, but it all begins with you!

I know what you must be thinking—not another test! Don't worry, though. Your teachers have been teaching you to read since you entered kindergarten, and with some determination you can do a great job! This book is going to be a big help to you in preparing for the test. It can be scary not knowing what to expect, but by the end of the book you will have a good understanding of this test, and that should ease your nerves!

Learning anything takes a lot of practice. When you practice, things become much easier. Have you ever tried to learn something new? Maybe you wanted to play a sport like basketball. In the beginning, you probably thought you would never be able to score any points. Through coaching and practice you were able to play better and gain more confidence. Then before you knew it, you were hitting that basket like a pro! Consider this book as your coach. You will get some pointers and tips on how to be successful on the PARCC. The helpful hints and sample tests included here will give you the confidence you need to do your very best work.

Keep in mind that the most important thing you can do is to read—a lot. Reading is cool, and you learn many new things by reading. In the assessments, you will be asked to read literature and informational texts, so try to read a balance of both. The best part about the PARCC is that the entire test is taken on the computer! That will certainly make it a lot more interesting, right? You will type all of your stories on the computer, so no more cramped hands while writing. As you practice, try to type some of your stories on the computer if you can. Becoming familiar with the keyboard and the functions of the computer will make things a lot easier and save time.

Common Core Overview

You probably have not given it much thought, but the work you are doing now is preparing you for your future college or career choices. Your parents and teachers are providing all the tools you will need to be successful in the future. Have you heard the term Common Core State Standards? These are guidelines that help your teachers and parents know what skills you will need in third grade to be successful in the future. You may be curious to know what exactly these standards are asking you to do to get you on the right path for college and careers. Basically, they are asking you to read both literature and informational text. They are also asking you to stretch yourself as a reader by reading a lot of challenging texts. This will help you grow as a reader. Good readers ask questions, think about what they read, and reread when they do not understand something. Reading challenging text will help you practice these good reading skills. The standards are also asking kids to provide evidence from the text when answering questions. You may have heard the term "text-based evidence." Going back to the text to find support for your answers will also help you develop into a good reader. In writing, the standards want you to practice with different types of writing. The three types of writing are opinion writing, informative and explanatory writing, and narrative writing. This book will help you determine how well you have mastered the standards in third grade. It will also provide you with some guidelines to help you through the process.

PARCC Overview

The PARCC assessment will determine your mastery of the Common Core State Standards. Please refer to the appendix in this book for a complete list of the ELA standards for Grade Three.

As a third grader, you will take an important test in the spring. The test is called the PARCC, which stands for Partnership for Assessment of Readiness for College and Careers. This test is an assessment given to students in grades three through twelve to determine how well they are mastering the standards. There's no need to be nervous, because your teachers have been providing you with the skills needed to do well on this assessment. Just as with anything, practicing will help you feel confident and will better prepare you for this important assessment. This book will help you, too!

PARCC Question Format

The PARCC assessment is taken on the computer. You will be asked to read passages and answer different types of questions on the computer.

There are three types of questions that you should become familiar with in order to be successful on the test.

1. **Evidence-Based Constructed-Response Question.** This is a multiple-choice question that has two parts. It is important to keep in mind that you must get Part A correct in order to score any points for Part B, since Part B depends on the answer choice you made for Part A. The good news is that you are allowed to go back to the story and reread the parts that may help you with the answer.

   Below is an example of an **Evidence-Based Constructed-Response** (EBCR) question. This is a type of multiple-choice question, which will have two parts.

Today you will read two stories titled "Johnny Chuck Finds the Best Thing in the World" and "Me First." As you read, think about the actions of the characters and the events of the stories. Answer the questions to help you write an essay.

Read the story titled "Johnny Chuck Finds the Best Thing in the World." Then answer the questions.

Johnny Chuck Finds the Best Thing in the World

by Thornton W. Burgess

1 Old Mother West Wind had stopped to talk with the Slender Fir Tree.

2 "I've just come across the Green Meadows," said Old Mother West Wind, "and there I saw the Best Thing in the World."

3 Striped Chipmunk was sitting under the Slender Fir Tree and he couldn't help hearing what Old Mother West Wind said. "The Best Thing in the World—now what can that be?" thought Striped Chipmunk. "Why, it must be heaps and heaps of nuts and acorns! I'll go and find it."

4 So Striped Chipmunk started down the Lone Little Path through the wood as fast as he could run. Pretty soon he met Peter Rabbit.

5 "Where are you going in such a hurry, Striped Chipmunk?" asked Peter Rabbit.

Part A

What does **cross** mean as it is used in paragraph 28 of "Johnny Chuck Finds the Best Thing in the World"?

- A. excited
- B. lost
- C. upset
- D. scared

Part B

Which statement **best** supports the answer to Part A?

- A. ". . . ran this way and ran that way . . ."
- B. ". . . hadn't found the Best Thing in the World."
- C. ". . . they started up the Lone Little Path . . . ."
- D. "They didn't hurry now . . . ."

Source: *parcconline.org*

2. **Technology-Enhanced Constructed-Response Question.** For this type of question, you will be asked to click, drag, highlight, and select answer choices. In the sample question below, you will be asked to click and drag three details from the story into the setting box at the bottom of the screen.

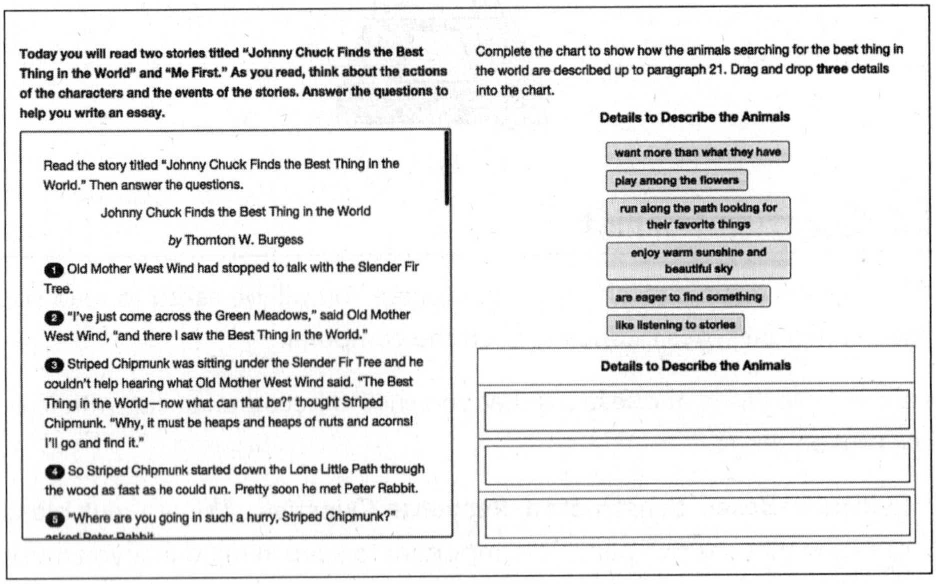

Source: *parcconline.org*

The example above shows a Technology-Enhanced Constructed-Response question. It is important to read the directions very careful when answering the question. This particular example refers you back to a specific paragraph to complete the question accurately.

3. **Prose Constructed-Response Question.** This writing task is connected directly to one or more texts that you will read. There are three types of prose constructed-response questions: narrative, literary analysis, and research simulation.

Sample Literacy Analysis Writing Task

The question below is an example of a Literary Analysis question. You will be asked to compare two stories that you will read and to type your response in the box below. A typical response to the question below would be in paragraph form. You must refer to the text to support your answer.

If you look at the tabs directly below the instructions, you will see a tab that says *Johnny Chuck Finds the Best Thing in the World* and a second tab labeled *Me First.* You will need to click on the tab to read each story in order to complete the essay. You will look at these tasks more closely as you work your way through this book. The size of the box that you need to type your story in may seem small, but as you type, the box scrolls down.

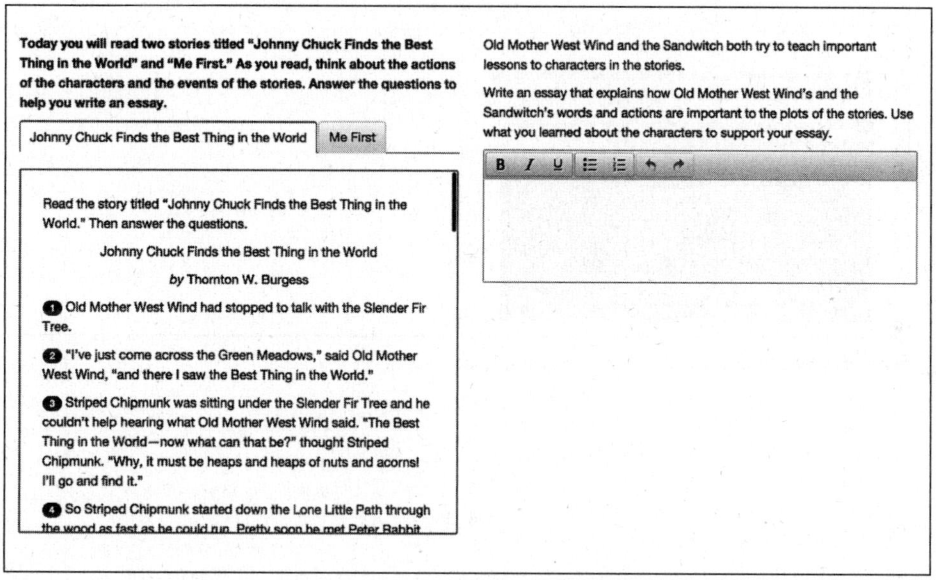

Source: *parcconline.org*

Sample Research Simulation Writing Task

In this example, you are asked to use the two texts to compare and contrast the key details about endangered animals and how they can be helped. Again, notice the two tabs that you will need to click on to read each story. The writing space may seem small, but as you write, the space will scroll down. Remember, you are writing an essay, not a short answer reply!

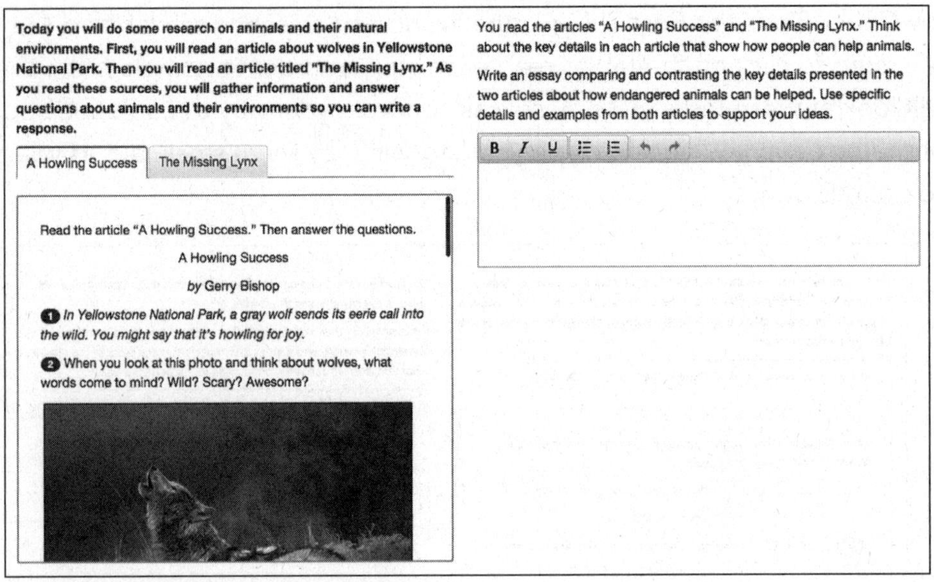

Source: *parcconline.org*

Sample Narrative Writing Task

In this task you are asked to write a journal entry from a character's point of view. Again, notice the box in which you will be writing your story. As you write, the box will scroll down. In this task, you will have only one story to read, so you won't see tabs above the story.

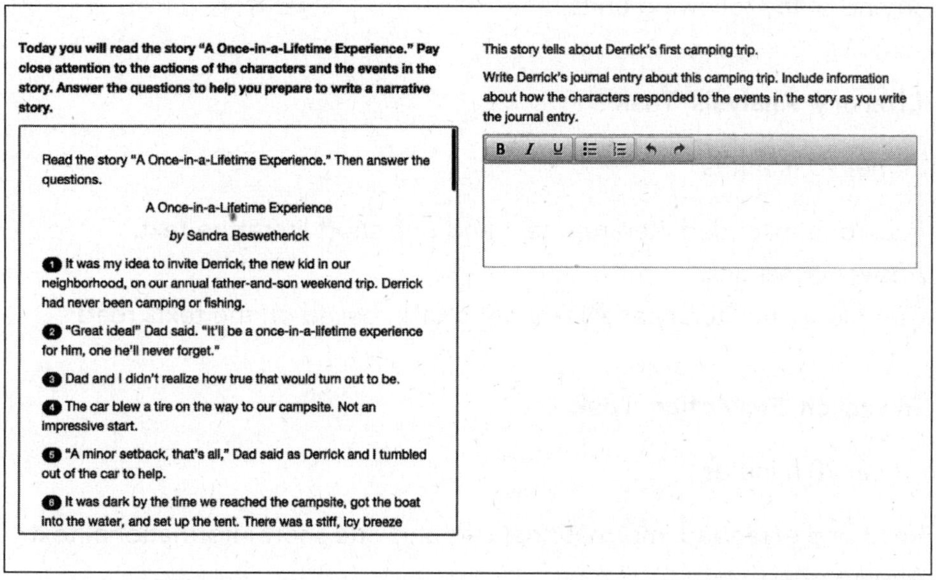

Today you will read the story "A Once-in-a-Lifetime Experience." Pay close attention to the actions of the characters and the events in the story. Answer the questions to help you prepare to write a narrative story.

Read the story "A Once-in-a-Lifetime Experience." Then answer the questions.

A Once-in-a-Lifetime Experience

by Sandra Beswetherick

1 It was my idea to invite Derrick, the new kid in our neighborhood, on our annual father-and-son weekend trip. Derrick had never been camping or fishing.

2 "Great idea!" Dad said. "It'll be a once-in-a-lifetime experience for him, one he'll never forget."

3 Dad and I didn't realize how true that would turn out to be.

4 The car blew a tire on the way to our campsite. Not an impressive start.

5 "A minor setback, that's all," Dad said as Derrick and I tumbled out of the car to help.

6 It was dark by the time we reached the campsite, got the boat into the water, and set up the tent. There was a stiff, icy breeze

This story tells about Derrick's first camping trip.

Write Derrick's journal entry about this camping trip. Include information about how the characters responded to the events in the story as you write the journal entry.

Source: *parcconline.org*

Testing Times and Format

Performance-Based Assessment

The Performance-Based Assessment will take place over three days. Each day will focus on one of the following units:

Unit: Literary Analysis Task

Unit time: 90 minutes

- Read one extended literature text and one short literature text.
- Answer questions.
- Complete one literary analysis writing task, based on the texts read.

Unit: Research Simulation Task

Unit time: 90 minutes

- Read one extended informational text and one short informational text.
- Answer questions.
- Complete one research simulation writing task, based on the texts read.

Unit: Narrative Writing Task

Unit time: 75 minutes

- Read one short text.
- Answer questions.
- Complete one narrative writing task, based on the text.

FAQ

Frequently Asked Questions

What will PARCC Assessments do?

The assessments will help determine whether you are mastering the standards. They will also provide your teachers and parents with important information on how well you are prepared for your college and career paths.

What types of questions does PARCC ask?

You will be expected to answer three types of questions: Evidence-Based Selected-Response, Technology-Enhanced Constructed-Response, and Prose Constructed-Response.

- Evidence-Based Selected-Response (EBSR) questions are multiple-choice, but all questions contain two parts. In Part A you will be asked a question, and in Part B you will be asked to support the answer you selected in Part A. It is essential that you understand that the correct answer in Part A will determine the correctness of Part B. Critical reading is very important.
- Technology-Enhanced Constructed-Response (TECR) questions are designed with the computer in mind. You may be asked to "drag and drop" sentences or words, highlight text, or select multiple items to provide an answer to a particular question.
- Prose Constructed-Response (PCR) questions require you to write—typically several paragraphs. The PCR question is related to the texts that you will read in the unit.

What can I do at home to help me prepare for the assessment?

There are a lot of things you can do at home to help get you prepared. First, make sure you find a quiet place to complete your homework in the evening. Also, make sure you read something each day. Try reading aloud to someone, too. Remember, the more you read, the better reader you will become! Try to read lots of different things, such as books, magazines, and newspapers. Ask questions as you read and try to visualize what is happening in the story. Make frequent trips to the library to select lots of interesting reading materials.

In addition, because the test is given on the computer, you should practice your typing skills as much as possible. Try typing some of the stories you write on the computer. If you do not have a computer at home, the library is a great place to practice those keyboarding skills!

How will this book help?

You will be introduced to strategies that will help you become familiar with the test format and gain confidence along the way. Checklists and rubrics (scoring guides for student writing) are provided and explained. These will help you understand what is expected and how the tests will be scored.

Opportunities for both guided and independent practice are available for each portion of the test. In the guided practice section, you are provided with information on how to tackle the question and some tips for doing a good job with the task. In the independent practice part, you will see how well you can do on your own. For additional practice, full sample tests for the Performance-Based Assessment and the End-of-Year Assessment are provided. The appendix contains additional information and resources.

You may be nervous that the test is timed. You may worry that time will run out before you finish. Practice tests, like the ones included in this book, are a good way to put these fears to rest. As you become more familiar with the test, you will build confidence and worry less.

Where can I get additional information about PARCC and the Common Core State Standards?

PARCC has a website that provides a wealth of information and resources for both educators and parents. Go to *http://www.parcconline.org*. For specific information about the standards, visit *http://www.corestandards.org*.

EBSR and TECR Questions

CHAPTER 1

Overview

You might be wondering why there are so many acronyms in the PARCC assessments. Do not let them confuse you; this book will help you make sense of them all. In this chapter, you are going to get an understanding of the two types of question formats that the PARCC will use. You will see these two types of questions in PARCC. It is important that you understand the questions. Here is an explanation of the terms.

EBSR stands for Evidence-Based Selected-Response.

This type of question has two parts. The first part, Part A, is multiple-choice. The second part of the question, Part B, asks you to use evidence from the text to prove your answer to the first part. If you do not get the first question correct, you will not receive any points for the second part. Think of these types of questions as piggyback questions because one question is connected to the other.

TECR stands for Technology-Enhanced Constructed-Response.

This type of question requires you to either drag and drop, cut and paste, or highlight responses. Sometimes the format will be a graphic organizer, a box, or a series of shapes in which to drag your answer. You can think of these types of questions as the "movable" responses because, more often than not, you will be moving the answers.

The most important thing you can do to score well on the PARCC assessment is to read the story or stories very carefully. If you have a good understanding of what you read, it will be easier to remember key concepts and ideas.

Good readers use multiple strategies to help them understand the text they are reading. Being an active reader will help you comprehend better. The more you practice these strategies, the quicker they will become automatic! Did you know that there are many different types of questions? Some questions are found right in the text, and others require you to use what you know and what you read to get the correct answer.

Types of Questions

Not all questions are the same. You should become familiar with the different types that may be asked in the EBSR and TECR questions. Below you will find examples of the types of questions asked.

Literal Comprehension Questions

You will find the answers to literal comprehension questions right in the text. All you need to do is locate the information from the selection. These types of questions are often called "right there" questions because the information is, well, right there!

Inferential Questions

Inferential questions are not found directly in the text. You can work out the answer with your own knowledge and experience by considering the hints and clues in the text. These questions will require you to draw conclusions on your own from the hints and clues that are given, but try not to completely make things up or jump to conclusions that are not supported by the text.

Thinking and Reasoning Questions

Thinking and reasoning questions may require you to think about the author's purpose, identify the main idea and key details, make predictions, or compare and contrast in order to determine the central message or point of view.

Vocabulary Questions

Vocabulary questions ask you to determine the meaning of words from their context in the text. It is important to remember that some words have more than one meaning. Be sure to read the sentence containing the vocabulary word as well as the surrounding sentences for clues to the word's meaning in the text. Pay attention to clues that come before or after the word to help you figure out how it is used in that selection.

Helpful Tips

Here are some ideas to keep in mind as you read. Good readers have strategies that help them understand what they read. You should use these strategies as you read.

What do good readers do?

- ☑ They monitor their own comprehension. This means that they notice when they do not understand something, so they stop reading and try to figure it out.
- ☑ They ask questions while they are reading.
- ☑ They make observations about the characters, setting, genre, or plot.
- ☑ They make predictions about what might happen next.
- ☑ They go back and reread when something is not clear.
- ☑ They visualize in their head what is happening.
- ☑ They infer things not directly stated in the text.

- ✔ They determine what is important and what is not.
- ✔ They recognize the author's purpose and the point of view.
- ✔ They analyze pictures and read captions or text boxes.

Okay, now you have a good idea of the different types of questions out there and what it means to be a good reader. That is a great start! You are probably feeling more confident already! As you go through this book, you will see lots of tips that will help you understand the tests. First are tips for answering multiple-choice questions.

Tips for Answering Multiple-Choice Questions

- ✔ Read the question carefully.
- ✔ Make sure you understand what the question is asking you to do.
- ✔ Look back in the text to find information that may help you answer the question.
- ✔ Read *all* answer choices, even if the first answer choice seems correct. In the PARCC there may be more than one choice that seems correct, but you will be asked to select the *best* answer!
- ✔ Don't try to be the first to finish. When you are done, check over your answers carefully.

Evidence-Based Selected-Response Format

The Evidence-Based Selected-Response (EBSR) format emphasizes the importance of Reading Standard 1 of the Common Core Standards:

Ask and answer questions to demonstrate understanding of a text, referring explicitly to the text as the basis for the answers.

EBSR questions always have two parts. The first part asks a standard question about the passage. The second part asks you to show evidence from the text that supports the answer you provided to the first question. Some questions on PARRC will ask you to select *two* answer choices for either Part A or Part B of the question. It is very important that you read the questions carefully in order to know how many selections you need to make.

Let's look at an example of the question format. Read the passage in the box below and answer the questions that follow. Be sure to read each question carefully.

> Molly looked at the moving truck outside her house. A tear ran down her cheek as she looked out her bedroom window. She had lived in this town all of her life. She loved the big tree outside of her house and the rocking chair on the porch. She would miss the flowers that she planted in the garden. Most of all, she would miss her best friend, Maria. Maria and Molly have been friends since first grade. She didn't want to move to a new town, but her father got another job and they had to go.

Part A

Which word **best** describes how the main character feels?

- O A. tired
- O B. worried
- O C. scared
- O D. unhappy

Notice that in Part A the question is asking which word **BEST** *describes the character's feelings. Keep in mind that more than one choice may describe the character's feelings, but you must decide on the* best choice. *The correct choice is letter D. The key details in the story best support that the character was feeling unhappy.*

Part B

Which two details from the passage best supports your answer?

- ☐ A. "She loved the big tree outside of her house and the rocking chair on the porch."
- ☐ B. "A tear ran down her cheek as she looked out her bedroom window."
- ☐ C. "Molly looked at the moving truck outside her house."
- ☐ D. "She didn't want to move to a new town, but her father got another job and they had to go."

Part B of the question is asking you to provide two key details (text evidence) that support the answer you chose for Part A. In Part A you answered "unhappy," so you will need to find the two details that support your answer. All the answer choices are found in the passage. It is important to read ALL the choices and think about which make the most sense. Letters B and D best support the answer that the main character was unhappy.

Let's Practice!

Now that you are familiar with the setup of the EBSR, let's practice!

Directions: Read this short practice text and answer the questions that follow. Keep in mind that the passages for PARCC will be longer and more complex. The purpose of this text is to provide guided practice with answering EBSR questions. The practice test at the end of this book will provide you with more in-depth passages that include a combination of EBSR and TECR and PCR writing tasks.

> Remember, you may look back at the reading passage to refresh your memory. Do not just guess the correct answer. If you are not sure of an answer, try locating the part of the text that may help you. Make sure you read all of your answer choices.

The Boy Who Cried Wolf

Folktale adapted from Aesop

1 There was once a boy who lived in a village up in the mountains. His family owned many sheep. The boy had a job, and that job was to watch the sheep. If a wolf came near, he needed to call for help. His sheep stayed on a hill near the village where he watched them every day.

2 One day, he thought of a trick he could play on the people who lived in the village. He was bored, so he thought this would be a way to have fun. He ran toward the village crying out loudly for help.

3 He shouted, "Wolf! Wolf! Come and help! The wolves are at my lambs! The wolves are trying to eat them!"

4 There were many villagers in the town. They heard him crying and thought that they had to help. So, the kind villagers left their work and ran to the field to help him. They would try to help him chase away the wolves and protect his lambs. However, when the villagers got there, the boy laughed at them. There was no wolf there. He just wanted to watch them come running! He thought it was funny.

5 Then another day the boy tried the same trick. Once again, the villagers came running to help him out, and once again the boy laughed at them.

6 Then, one day, a wolf really did come and it started chasing the lambs! **Frantically**, the boy ran for help. Desperate with fear he cried, "Wolf! Wolf! There is a wolf! Help! Please! Help! Please!"

7 All the villagers heard him, but this time they did not come. They thought he was pulling another mean trick. They had learned their lesson and did not need to be laughed at again. So, no one paid attention to him and the shepherd boy lost all his sheep—they all ran away!

8 When people in the village found out what had happened, they were sorry, but they told the boy it was his fault. This is the kind of thing that happens to people who are untruthful. When you continue to lie, people will not believe you, even when you tell the truth.

Questions

Part A

What is the **best** meaning of the word **frantically** as it is used in paragraph 6?

Hint: Go back and reread paragraph 6.

- O A. careful
- O B. calm
- O C. angry
- O D. worried

Part B

Which detail from the story **best** supports the answer to Part A?

O A. "So, the kind villagers left their work and ran to the field to help him." (paragraph 4)

O B. "Desperate with fear he cried, 'Wolf! Wolf! There is a wolf! Help! Please! Help! Please!'" (paragraph 6)

O C. "The boy had a job, and that job was to watch the sheep." (paragraph 1)

O D. "He was bored, so he thought this would be a way to have fun." (paragraph 2)

Hint: Think about your answer for Part A. Which letter choice best supports that answer?

Answers

Part A. The correct answer is D. At the end of the story the boy was finally telling the truth, but no one would listen and this worried him greatly. He was worried the sheep would be killed by the wolves.

Part B. The correct answer is B. The statement *Desperate with fear he cried, "Wolf! Wolf! There is a wolf! Help! Please! Help! Please!"* best supports that the boy was worried.

Not all EBCR will be based on vocabulary; some questions may ask you about character traits, about motivations or feelings, or the central or main ideas and the key details. Remember, there may be both literal and inferential questions; be sure you know the difference between the two. Additionally, the texts may be literary or informational. All questions will ask you for evidence to support your answer.

Use details from the story "The Boy Who Cried Wolf" to answer the following questions. Remember, you may go back and reread the story.

Questions

Part A

What is the central message of "The Boy Who Cried Wolf"?

- O A. Always try your best.
- O B. Be kind to others.
- O C. Always tell the truth.
- O D. Beauty is in the eye of the beholder.

Part B

Which detail from the story supports this message?

- O A. "He was bored, so he thought this would be a way to have fun." (paragraph 2)
- O B. "His sheep stayed on a hill near the village where he watched them every day." (paragraph 1)
- O C. "When you continue to lie, people will not believe you, even when you tell the truth." (paragraph 8)
- O D. "They would try to help him chase away the wolves and protect his lambs." (paragraph 4)

Answers

Part A. The correct answer for Part A is C. For this question you are asked to determine the central message. You will need to ask yourself, "What is the big idea or lesson the writer is trying to teach me?" The key details in the story support the central idea, to "always tell the truth."

Part B. The correct answer for Part B is C. *When you continue to lie, people will not believe you, even when you tell the truth.* This detail supports the central idea to always tell the truth. Although choices A, B, and D are found in the story, they do not support that central idea.

Technology-Enhanced Constructed-Response Format

Now we will take a close look at another type of multiple-choice question you will encounter on the PARCC. Technology-Enhanced Constructed-Response (TECR) questions will require you to use the computer to drag and drop, to copy and paste, or to highlight answers. Sometimes the format will be a graphic organizer, a box, or a series of shapes in which to drag your answer.

For practice purposes, you will write your answer in this book. Becoming familiar with the format will really help you when you take the real test. Again, just as with the EBSR questions, you will need to read the question carefully and think about what it is asking.

Go back to the story to make sure you remembered the key details. There may seem to be more than one correct answer to some of the questions. Remember, you are selecting the *best* answer to the question. You will need to provide text evidence for your answers. The most important thing to do is to read the text thoughtfully and carefully. Make sure you understand what you are reading by practicing what good readers do when they read.

Sample TECR Question

Let's look at a sample TECR question. This sample question asks you to select **one** main idea and write it in the box below labeled Main Idea. You are then asked to choose **two** details that best support the main idea. Write each detail into the box labeled Supporting Details.

Directions: Read the story "George Washington Carver" and think about the main idea of the article. Select the best answer for the main idea and write it in the box below the heading labeled Main Idea. Select two supporting details for the main idea you selected. Write the two supporting details in each box.

George Washington Carver

1 George Washington Carver lived from 1864 to 1943. He spent much of his life helping farmers to use their land in better ways. His ideas have helped farmers in many countries around the world.

2 Carver was in charge of farm research at Tuskegee Institute, a college in Alabama. He taught students how to farm. He also worked with southern farmers on their land. In the southern part of the United States, most farmers had grown cotton for so many years that the soil had worn out. Carver showed them how to improve the land.

3 Carver said the farmers should plant peanuts. Peanuts would enrich the soil. Farmers asked who would buy so many peanuts if they planted them. Carver answered by finding more than 300 new ways to use peanuts. Farmers could feed the vines to farm animals. They could use the hulls for fertilizer. Carver even found a way to make paper from the peanut shells.

4 When Carver died, he left his money to help people to keep working on farm research. Today, people from many countries come to the George Washington Carver Foundation at Tuskegee Institute. There they learn better ways of farming.

Used with permission from *DePaul University Center for Urban Education*

Sample question: Select the answer that **best** states the main idea from the article you read and write it under the heading "Main Idea."

Possible Main Ideas

Carver helped farmers find better ways to use their land.
Carver enjoyed being a farmer and loved peanuts..
Carver started the Washington Carver Foundation.

Note: On a computerized test you may be asked to click and drag the correct response into the box labeled Main Idea, or the response may appear on a drop-down menu. You may also be asked to go back to the text and highlight passages.

Possible Supporting Details

They could use the hulls for fertilizer.
George Washington Carver lived from 1864 to 1943.
Farmers could feed the vines to farm animals.
Carver was in charge of farm research at Tuskegee Institute.

Select one main idea and two key details to complete the chart below.

Main Idea
Supporting Detail
Supporting Detail

Now that you are familiar with the setup of the TECR, let's practice!

Let's Practice!

Read this short practice text and answer the questions that follow. Keep in mind that the passages for PARCC will be longer and more complex. The purpose of this text is to provide guided practice with answering TECR questions. The practice test at the end of this book will provide you with more in-depth passages that include a combination of EBSR and TECR and PCR writing tasks.

A Better Community

1 My daughter Anna brought a note home. I looked at the note and smiled. "So we will have a recycling center," I said. She started to explain why it is important to recycle. "I know," I said, "but I don't have time."

2 Anna thought of a way to recycle. She set up a bag in the kitchen. She said it would be for plastic. We would put plastic in there. Then, once a month we would take the plastic to the Recycle Center. She said that plastic takes a lot of energy to make. And she said that it is hard for the environment when people throw it out.

3 It seemed like a good idea, but then the bag got full. In one week we had filled it with empty plastic bottles.

4 My daughter said we should look at what we use. We are using too much plastic. So we looked for ways to use less plastic.

5 I told my neighbor about this. She liked the idea. She started keeping her plastic in a bag. We all went together to the Recycle Center on the first Saturday. We brought our plastic.

6 When we got there, we saw many bags. People had brought lots of trash. They brought paper and metal, too. "Now that we have this center, it is easier to recycle," said my neighbor.

Used with permission from *DePaul University Center for Urban Education*

Directions: In the box below, write a character trait that **best** describes the daughter in "A Better Community." Select one choice from the list of character traits below and write it in the box below labeled Character Trait. Then select two details that support the trait you selected and write them in the boxes below labeled Supporting Detail 1 and Supporting Detail 2.

Character Traits	Supporting Details
Caring	The mother smiled at the note.
Silly	Anna thought of a way to recycle.
Selfish	The neighbors were at the recycling center.
Angry	Anna set up a bag in the kitchen.
	People did not want the recycling center.

Character Trait
Supporting Detail 1
Supporting Detail 2

Answers

Character Trait
Caring
Supporting Detail 1
Anna thought of a way to recycle.
Supporting Detail 2
Anna set up a bag in the kitchen.

The correct character trait choice is "caring." Anna was caring because she thought of a way to recycle and she set up a bag in the kitchen. These details support the character trait of someone who is caring. The choices of silly, selfish, or angry do not have sufficient text evidence. Remember, the directions state to select the *best* trait.

Let's try another text.

Directions: Today you will read an article called "A Frog's Life" about the life cycle of a frog. Read the passage carefully and choose the **best** answer for each question. You may look back at the passages as often as necessary.

A Frog's Life

1 Frogs are found throughout the world except in very cold places. They are most common in rain forests. Frogs are amphibians, meaning that they can live in water or on land. Most frogs spend most of their lives in water.

2 When you were born, your family and friends saw how much you looked like your mother or your father. Perhaps your eyes are the same shape as your dad's. Or maybe your chin looks just like your mom's. Well, no one ever said those things about a baby frog. A baby frog does not look anything like an adult frog. In fact, baby frogs are not even called frogs! They are called tadpoles.

Life Begins in an Egg

3 Frogs lay their eggs in water or wet places. The eggs are in a jellylike substance and clump together. This large clump of eggs is called frog spawn. Some frogs can lay more than 1,000 eggs. Only a few of the eggs will survive to grow into adult frogs.

4 Life for a frog begins when a single cell inside the egg begins to split. Each surviving egg is called an embryo. The life that is now growing in the egg looks like a tadpole. In three weeks the tadpole will hatch with gills, a mouth, and a tail.

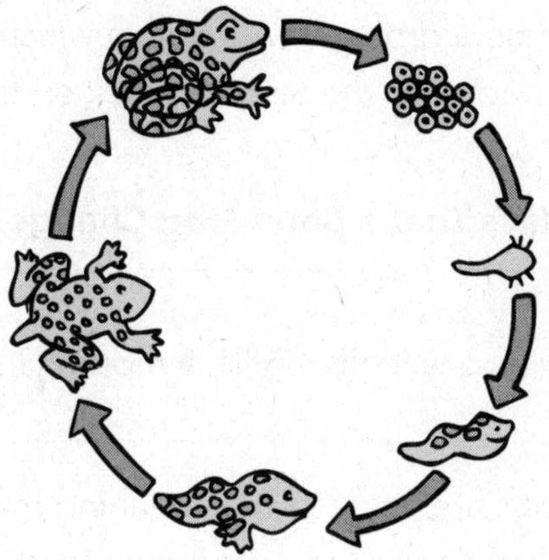

The Tadpole Begins to Change

5 In five weeks the tadpole begins another cycle of change. First, it starts to grow legs. Next, the lungs begin to develop. The front legs will begin to grow before the tail disappears. The tadpole is now called a froglet. It looks like a tiny frog with a tail! Just a few more weeks and the cycle will be complete. Sixteen weeks after hatching, the frog has gone through a complete growth cycle.

Difference Between the Life Cycle of Frogs and Toads

6 Toads also lay their eggs in water because their babies start off as tadpoles, just like frog babies do. The difference is that frog eggs are laid in bunches and they have a jellylike substance around them. Toads lay their eggs in lines, or strands, on leaves of plants that live in the water.

From *New York State Grade 3 Elementary-Level English Language Arts Test,* by Jane A. Gallant (Barron's, 2008)

TECR Question 1

Complete the chart to show **two** ways a baby frog changes before it completes the growth cycle and becomes an adult frog.

Note: *On a computer you may be asked to drag and drop your choices into the correct box. There may also be a drop-down menu in which to make your selection or you may be asked to go back into the text and click on the correct sentence.*

Ways That a Baby Frog Changes

The baby frog will grow gills, a mouth, and a tail.
Frogs are amphibians, meaning that they can live in water or on land.
Lungs will begin to develop when it is a tadpole.
Most frogs spend most of their lives in water.

Ways That a Baby Frog Changes

Answer to TECR Question 1

Ways That a Baby Frog Changes

The baby frog will grow gills, a mouth, and a tail.
Frogs are amphibians, meaning that they can live in water or on land.
Lungs will begin to develop when it is a tadpole.
Most frogs spend most of their lives in water.

Ways That a Baby Frog Changes

The baby frog will grow gills, a mouth, and a tail.
Lungs will begin to develop when it is a tadpole.

The baby frog will grow gills, a mouth, and a tail and *Lungs will begin to develop when it is a tadpole* are the statements that describe how a baby frog changes during development. Although the statements, "Frogs are amphibians, meaning that they can live in water or on land" and "Most frogs spend most of their lives in water" are mentioned in the story, they do not describe how a frog changes.

Good readers are able to read *all* the answers and decide which choices make sense for the question being asked. Do not be fooled by choices that may appear in the passage but that do not answer the questions!

TECR Question 2

The article describes the differences between frogs and toads. Use details from the article to complete the following chart. Select a key detail that supports ways they are alike and ways they are different. Write the key details to complete the graphic organizer.

Key Details

Eggs laid in lines

Babies are tadpoles

Eggs laid in bunches

Frogs	Both	Toads

Note: *On a computer you may be asked to drag and drop your choices into the correct box.*

Answer to TECR Question 2

The article states in the last paragraph that both frogs and toads have babies that are called tadpoles. A frog will lay eggs in bunches and a toad will lay eggs in lines. Be sure to reread the section before answering the question. You may also take notes as you read to help you remember the facts. Remember, as you read look for key words or phrases such as "just like," which compares or tells how they are alike, and "one difference," which contrasts or shows differences.

Frogs	Both	Toads
Eggs laid in bunches	Babies are tadpoles	Eggs laid in lines

CHAPTER 2

Narrative Writing Task

Overview

The Narrative Writing Task is something you may be familiar with doing in your classroom. The word "narrative" simply means a story. Narrative writing can be used to tell about experiences or events, real or imaginary. In this task, you may be asked to write a story, detail a scientific process, write a historical account of important figures, or describe an account of events, scenes, or objects. You may see a Prose Constructed-Response (PCR) question on the test. A PCR question is a fancy way of asking you to write a story or an essay. This sounds simple enough, right? There is a catch, though. You must first read a short text and then answer some questions about the story you just read. You will answer EBSR or TECR items and then you will be asked to write a story.

Here is a recap of the Narrative Writing Tasks and the order you will see them on the test:

- ☑ Read a short literary text.
- ☑ Answer EBSR or TECR items.
- ☑ Write a narrative story (PCR).

This book will provide you with some practice on the types of questions you may be asked to write on the PARCC. Remember, you will always read a text first! It is important to read the story very carefully. This will help you when you get to the questions. You will also have a highlight tool to use as you read and to reference important parts in the story as you reread. It might be helpful to practice using the highlighting tool before the test. Remember to highlight only important parts! Some students overuse this tool. You can always go back to the story if it helps.

Format for Response

When you read the narrative writing task you will need to think about what it is asking you to produce. Will you have to write a letter, a diary entry, or maybe an ending to the story you just read? The chart below gives you some ideas on what the narrative writing task may ask you to produce in your writing response. The story you read will be a jumping-off point for your writing. As you practice with narrative writing tasks, always ask yourself, "What format is the prompt asking me to respond in?"

Adventure/Short stories	Autobiography	Biography
Book reviews	Brochures	Character sketches
Descriptions	Diaries	Speeches
Endings	Essays	Explanations
Fables	Fantasy stories	Fiction
Reports	Humorous stories	Magazine articles
Letters	Science articles	Pamphlets
News articles	Sequels	Reviews

Note: Additional formats may be on the actual test.

It is important to recognize which format to use. A sequel format would look very different from a letter format. After you read the directions, write down the key words to let you know what format you are going to use. Be sure to stick to that format throughout your writing.

Opening Your Story

When you think about how to begin your writing response there are things you should keep in mind. One thing good writers do is make sure the first few lines of their story are interesting enough to grab the reader's attention. The opening lines are important to set the tone for your story. The chart below provides some ideas on ways you can open your story.

Start with . . .	Example
a Question	Have you ever wanted something so much that it's all you could think about?
a Setting	The room was dark and shadows seemed to flicker on the walls. The wind began to howl through the only window in the room.
an Exclamation	"Help! I'm down here," replied a small voice from under the porch.
Dialogue	"I've made some cookies for tea," said Ma.
a Description of the Weather	The pitter patter of raindrops bounced against my window. I could see puddles beginning to form as the sky turned a smoky gray.
a Sense of Action	Something moved behind her. She turned, frightened. The night was too dark. She couldn't see anything. There it was again!

Another thing to consider is the point of view from which you will write your story. Point of view basically lets the reader know who is telling the story. When you are reading the directions for the writing task, make sure you understand which format to use for your response. Once you know the format, you can figure out the point of view you need to write from. The chart below will give you some tips for determining from which point of view you will begin to write your story.

Point of View

You must know that a narrator is the character who tells a story. Who will be telling your story? Does the question ask you to take on a specific role of a character or will you be telling the story as someone who is not in the story? For example:

Diary: For this format you may be asked to take on the role of a character in the story or write an entry from another person's perspective.

Fable: For this format you would be telling the story as an outsider, meaning you would not place yourself in the story.

It is helpful to be able to know the different points of view that a writer might need to take on as he or she writes. This can help you as you begin to plan your narrative response.

Point of View Based on PARCC Writing Format		
Point of View	**List of Pronouns**	**Samples of Formats**
1st Person You are the speaker in the story.	I, me, myself, we, us, ourselves, ours, mine	• Personal narratives • Diary Entry • Autobiography • Reviews • Writing as if you were a character in the story • Letters • Opinion
2nd Person You address an audience without placing yourself in the writing.	you, yours, yourself, yourselves	• Speeches • Directions • Pamphlets • Procedural
3rd Person Describes how characters think and feel. Does not take part in the event.	he, she, it, its, him, her, his, hers, himself, herself, itself, they, them, their, theirs, themselves	• Summary/Response • Compare/Contrast • Descriptive narrative • Research • Fables • Fiction

To help with the overall flow, you will need to map out the plot or sequence of events of the story. Before writing, think about what you will have at the beginning, middle, and end. You may want to sketch a quick plot graph to help you organize your writing. Since you will not have a lot of time, you may want to use a box-and-bullet format.

Here are some guidelines:

1. Make a box for the beginning.
2. In the box, write what happens in the beginning.
3. Below the box, put bullets telling how you show that event (sensory details, dialogue, and so on).
4. Repeat for the middle and the end.

Beginning

While at the beach I discovered something shining in the sand.

- I could see the foamy waves crashing over it.
- It sparkled like diamonds in the sand.
- I shouted, "Mom, I think I may have found something!"

Middle

I reached the spot where it was, only to discover that the waves had buried it into the sand.

- I quickly used my hands as a shovel.
- I could feel the wet sand rubbing against my hands.
- My heart pounded as I got closer.

End

I finally found my treasure . . . a bottle cap!

- I shrugged my shoulders and looked down.
- "Better luck next time!" my mom yelled.

A little planning in the beginning will help you keep your writing organized. You will be allowed to have a paper and pencil next to you during the test, but you will need to type your story on the computer.

You will need a handy set of linking words and phrases to use in your writing. Linking words and phrases really help to add a nice organizational flow to your story. Remember to include these words and phrases in your writing. Some examples of linking words and phrases are *first, next, then, finally, after, last, before,* and *later.*

Details, Details, Details

The box-and-bullet format will help give you a quick plan for your writing, but you will need to develop the details. Include detailed descriptions about the character's thoughts, actions, and feelings. Don't just say he was angry. That doesn't help the reader visualize what he looked like. Instead, write a description showing the actions of being angry. "He clenched his fist, and his face turned red as he stomped out of the room." Now that description would let the reader know he was angry and would help the reader to visualize it. This technique is called showing, not telling. Here are a few examples of showing versus telling sentences. Think about which one you think sounds better.

Telling	Showing
She walked home in the wind.	The wind whipped across her face as she leaned in trying to fight it off. She could hear the wind whistling through the empty streets.
The steam engine was moving fast.	Dirt was flying everywhere, and the smoke and steam were so thick that the people could hardly see anything.
I was really excited and nervous.	I kept going to the window every five seconds to check and see if the taxi had arrived. I was so jumpy that when the phone rang I nearly fell off my chair!
The classroom was a mess.	Books, papers, and tools were strewn everywhere across the classroom, making the place look rather like a teenager's bedroom.

Be sure to make your writing stand out by using showing rather than telling sentences. Include dialogue in your story, too. When characters have a voice in the story, it makes them come alive!

Ending Your Story

The ending of your story is just as important as the beginning. All stories need a sense of closure. Also remember to use linking words and phrases as you are approaching the end of your story.

Here are some ways that writers bring their stories to an end.

End with . . .	Example
an Exclamation	*The frog excitedly hopped away and wondered what new adventures tomorrow would bring!* **For a journal or diary entry writing task:** *I excitedly skipped away and wondered what new adventures tomorrow would bring!*
a Universal Word This technique uses a universal word in the last sentence or two, such as: *every, everything, everyone, all, always, we, us,* and *all the world.*	*Maria would <u>always</u> remember the special times she had with her grandfather.* **For a journal or diary entry writing task:** *I would <u>always</u> remember the special times I had with my grandfather.*
Advice to the Reader	*If you lose the big game, try not to worry. Remember, the important thing is not whether you win or lose, but how you played the game!* **For a journal or diary entry writing task:** (You would not give advice to the reader if this was a journal or diary entry, but you may reflect on a lesson) *I sure hope my sister learned her lesson because it doesn't matter whether you win or lose, it's how you play the game!*
a Lesson or Moral	*Remember that little friends may prove to be great friends.* **For a journal or diary entry writing task:** *I learned an important lesson about friendship, and I will never make that mistake again!*

Student Checklist

NARRATIVE WRITING CHECKLIST FOR GRADE 3

- [ ] I understood the format of the task.
- [ ] I described the narrator and/or characters.
- [ ] I planned an opening that will show readers what is going on.
- [ ] My opening sentences introduce readers to my narrator and/or characters.
- [ ] I used dialogue to show the character's thoughts and feelings.
- [ ] I included showing, not telling, sentences in my writing.
- [ ] I used temporal words or phrases to signal event order.
- [ ] I included my characters' responses to events in the story.
- [ ] I planned for how my story or narrative will end.
- [ ] I spent enough time planning this narrative or story.

Scoring Rubric

Okay, let's discuss how the writing will be scored. All of the writing components in PARCC will use a rubric. A rubric is a scoring tool used to measure the quality of a piece of writing. A rubric can also help you know what the expectation is for the writing assignment. The high end of the rubric lets you know what you would need to have in your writing to get a great score. The low end of the rubric lets you know the things you want to try to avoid when writing. You can consider a rubric as a guide to great writing. Be sure to look in the appendix for the complete rubric used to score the PARCC writing tasks.

Writing **Knowledge of Language and Conventions**	The student response to the prompt demonstrates **full command** of the conventions of standard English at an appropriate level of complexity. There **may** be a **few minor errors** in mechanics, grammar, and usage, but **meaning is clear**. **Note:** This means your spelling, punctuation, capitalization, grammar, and paragraphing needs to be good. Spelling and punctuation should be correct to help with the flow of your story. Try varying the kinds of sentences you write to include exclamations, questions, and showing, not telling, sentences. Capitalization should be used correctly. Paragraphing the beginning, middle, and end of your story will help with organization.

Remember to:

- ✔ Make sure your story is addressing the task.
- ✔ Establish a situation and introduce a narrator and/or characters; organize an event sequence that unfolds naturally.
- ✔ Be sure your story has an organized flow. The use of temporal words will help in having a clear beginning, middle, and end to your writing.
- ✔ Use dialogue and descriptions of actions, thoughts, and feelings to develop experiences and events or to show the response of characters to situations.
- ✔ Provide a sense of closure.

It is a good idea to do some planning before writing your story. You can use scratch paper or the online notepad to map out your story. A little planning will help you as you write.

Let's Practice!

Now that you have some guidelines to help ease you through the narrative writing task, it is time to practice!

During the actual test you will be given more TECR and EBSR questions and longer texts. The purpose of this chapter is to provide practice with the writing tasks, so the texts have been kept shorter and only a couple of questions have been provided.

The practice test at the end of this book will provide you with a full set of questions and more in-depth passages that provide a complete overview of the Narrative Task expectations.

Remember, in this task you are allowed to go back into the story to help you!

Directions: You will read a story below called "Roger Plans for a Snow Day." As you read, pay close attention to the plot of the story and how characters react to situations. After you have finished reading the story, you will answer questions and prepare to write a narrative story.

Roger Plans for a Snow Day

1 I don't usually watch the weather report, but tonight is different. Tomorrow could be the day. I had to find out for myself.

2 There was a buzz of excitement in the halls at school today. Everyone was hoping the big storm would come during the night. If the storm did come, we could get more than 36 inches of snow. That is more than 3 feet of snow. My kid sister is only 3 feet tall. The snow could be over her head!

3 I have never seen that much snow. I have lived in Florida most of my life. My family moved to the Adirondack Mountains last summer. This will be my first snowstorm.

4 The weatherman just said there is a 95 percent chance the storm will hit our area. It will start late tonight and end by dinnertime tomorrow. We could really have a snow day.

5 I called my three best friends. I needed to know what to do if it snows all day. We made our plans right away. Jimmy decided that we should all spend the night at his house. This way, no one will have to walk or ask their parents to drive during the snowstorm in the morning. We would all bring our sleeping bags, a favorite inside game, and our outside winter clothes.

6 All I had to do now was convince my parents to let me stay at Jimmy's house tonight. I can hear their thoughts now. "But tomorrow is a school day. What if the weather report is incorrect?" I prepared my answers. Tomorrow could be a great day!

7 I got myself ready. I went downstairs with my sleeping bag, my favorite indoor game, my outside winter clothes, and my hopes that I could convince my parents to let me go to Jimmy's house. I did not expect the surprise waiting for me in the family room!

8 I was greeted by my three best friends. Each had a sleeping bag, their favorite indoor game, and their outside winter clothes. My parents had arranged for them all to spend the night at my house. My parents said they wanted me to enjoy my very first snow day playing in my new house with my new best friends.

From *New York State Grade 3 Elementary-Level English Language Arts Test,* by Jane A. Gallant (Barron's, 2008)

1. **Part A.** How does Roger feel about the approaching storm?

O A. unhappy
O B. excited
O C. terrified
O D. calm

Part B. What detail from the text best supports your answer for question 1?

O A. "Tomorrow could be a great day!" (paragraph 6)
O B. "The weatherman just said there is a 95 percent chance the storm will hit our area." (paragraph 4)
O C. "I was greeted by my three best friends." (paragraph 8)
O D. "My family moved to the Adirondack Mountains last summer." (paragraph 3)

2. **Part A.** Read paragraph 1 from the story in the box below.

> I don't usually watch the weather report, but tonight is different. Tomorrow could be the day. I had to find out for myself.

What does "Tomorrow could be the day" mean as used in the story?

O A. Roger is moving from Florida.
O B. Roger is starting school.
O C. A storm would be coming.
O D. Roger would have a sleepover.

Part B. What detail from the story supports your answer to Part A?

O A. "I called my three best friends." (paragraph 5)
O B. "Everyone was hoping the big storm would come during the night." (paragraph 2)
O C. "All I had to do now was convince my parents to let me stay at Jimmy's house tonight." (paragraph 6)
O D. "My family moved to the Adirondack Mountains last summer." (paragraph 3)

3. Part A. Based on the story you just read, how did Roger's parents react to the approaching storm?

O A. They were worried.
O B. They were excited for Roger.
O C. They did not care one way or another.
O D. They were upset.

Part B. What happens in the story that best supports your answer to Part A?

O A. They surprised Roger by having his friends sleep over at their house.
O B. They told Roger to go sleep at a neighbor's house.
O C. They wanted to move back to Florida.
O D. They decided not to go to work the next day.

4. Part A. Based on the story you just read, why do the friends think a sleepover is a good idea?

O A. They have never had a sleepover.
O B. They want to stay up late.
O C. They are worried about asking their parents to drive the next day.
O D. They want to play video games.

Part B. What details from the text support your answer choice to Part A?

O A. "This way, no one will have to walk or ask their parents to drive during the snowstorm in the morning." (paragraph 5)
O B. "The weatherman just said there is a 95 percent chance the storm will hit our area." (paragraph 4)
O C. "Everyone was hoping the big storm would come during the night." (paragraph 2)
O D. "This will be my first snowstorm." (paragraph 3)

5. In the box below write the correct answer for the feeling that Roger had about the sleepover at the end of the story.

Feeling	

O A. Tired
O B. Angry
O C. Surprised
O D. Disappointed

Answers

1. The correct answer for Part A is choice B. "Roger feels excited about the snow day." In the story Roger is looking forward to spending the day with his friends.

   The correct answer for Part B is choice A, "Tomorrow could be a great day!" This answer choice best shows that Roger was excited about the snow day.

2. The correct answer for Part A is choice C, "A storm would be coming." The details in paragraph 1 discuss weather. Remember to use context clues when you are not sure of an answer. Also keep in mind that some of the answer choices are events that happened in the story, but that do not support the sentence, "Tomorrow could be a great day!"

   The correct answer for Part B is choice B, "Everyone was hoping the big storm would come during the night." This answer best supports Roger thinking, "Tomorrow could be the day."

3. The correct answer for Part A is choice B, "They were excited for Roger." There is no evidence from the story that supports that Roger's parents were worried, uncaring, or upset. They arranged for the sleepover; therefore, you can infer that at the end of the story they were excited for Roger.

   The correct answer for Part B is choice A, "They surprised Roger by having his friends sleep over at their house." This statement best supports that they were excited for Roger.

4. The correct answer for Part A is choice C, "They are worried about asking their parents to drive the next day." Do not be tricked by answer choices that seem correct; you must use text evidence when asking questions. They may want to play video games and stay up late, but the *text* does not say that is the reason for wanting a sleepover.

   The correct answer for Part B is choice A, "This way, no one will have to walk or ask their parents to drive during the snowstorm in the morning." This is directly stated in the text as the *main* reason for the sleepover.

5.

Feeling	*Surprised*

   Roger originally thought he would be sleeping over at his friend's house. When he came down the stairs he was surprised that his parents had arranged a sleepover at his house.

Narrative Writing Task

You have just read the story, "Roger Plans for a Snow Day." Write a story that continues where the passage ended. Be sure to tell what happens next using what you have learned from the story about the characters and the setting.

Guidelines for Answering the Narrative Task

First, ask yourself what the format is that you will be using. Write the format on the line below:

Format for task: --

Next, ask yourself what point of view you will write from. What words will you use?

Point of view: ---

Create a quick box-and-bullet plan for your writing:

Beginning	**Middle**	**End**
Details	**Details**	**Details**
•	•	•

Briefly outline what will happen in the next part of the story. Refer back to the charts in this chapter for additional support. In the bulleted section, jot down some sensory details. **Sensory details** include sight, sound, touch, smell, and taste. If you want your reader to visualize what is happening, using sensory details will help. In order to help the reader connect to your characters, use character descriptions, feelings, and reactions to events. Use this format to help guide your writing.

Here's how your answers to these guidelines might look.

First, ask yourself what the format is that you will be using. Write the format on the line below:

Format for task: Sequel

This task is asking you to imagine what would come next in the story. In order to do this you would need to use the same characters and develop the plot. So far you know that Roger is having a sleepover at his house, three of his friends are staying over, and his parents arranged for the sleepover. You also know that a big snowstorm is supposed to come. As you look back in the story, you can tell that it is written from Roger's point of view.

Next, ask yourself what point of view you will write from. What words will you use?

Point of view: First person (I, me, we)

Because Roger is telling the story, not an outside narrator, it's written from his point of view, which is the first person.

Sample Box-and-Bullet Outline

Wow! I shouted. This is going to be the best sleepover yet!

- I could smell the delicious chocolate chip cookies my mom was baking.
- As we set up our sleeping bags, tiny white snowflakes began to fall.
- We rushed to the back door and looked up at the frozen sky.

After that, we played board games and fell asleep.

- Everyone was so excited—we could barely focus on the games.
- We could see the snow gently falling.
- After several hours we all finally fell asleep

Finally, we woke up, and everything seemed so quiet.

- I looked outside and saw the white, glistening snow pressed up against the window.
- My neighborhood was transformed into a white winter wonderland!

Keep in mind that your bullets do not necessarily have to be written in sentence form. You could just jot down a couple of words to remember. The box-and-bullets will not be scored. They are used only to help guide you in your writing. The more you use them, the quicker you will get. You may want to include temporal words in the middle and ending paragraphs to keep the story in sequence.

Next, you can think about how you would like to start your story. What descriptive details will you include? How can you make a telling sentence into a showing sentence? Add some dialogue, too! Don't forget to use some of the ending techniques discussed in this chapter.

Here is a sample of what a response may look like using some of the techniques mentioned:

As I looked at my friends standing by the doorway, I shouted, "Wow, this is going to be the best sleepover ever!" I was so excited, and my friends were, too. We all high-fived each other.

Mom said, "Why don't you all go into the living room while I put some cookies into the oven." My friend James brought the game Battleship and another friend brought a video game! We stopped when mom told us the cookies were ready. Then we headed to the kitchen for some cold milk and warm cookies. The next thing we knew, snowflakes were falling from the sky. My friend James shouted, "Woo-hoo! It looks like no school for us tomorrow!"

After we finished, we decided to put on some of our snow gear. The snow was coming down fast and it would be a great time to try to build my first snowball ever! We all put on our snow boots, jackets, gloves, and hats. My mother shouted, "Be careful now!"

"We will," everyone yelled. I couldn't wait to scoop up some snow and form it into a ball. Suddenly, we had a snowball fight going on! It was so much fun! We decided to head back in and get changed out of our wet clothes.

When I woke up the next morning, everything seemed so quiet. I looked out the window while my friends continued to sleep. I slipped back into my sleeping bag with a smile on my face. I will always remember my first snowfall!

Note: Not everything you write in your box-and-bullet outline needs to be used in your writing. The purpose is to give you a map for your writing. You may decide to add different details or eliminate one of your ideas. The important thing is to keep writing!

Once you have completed your writing, go back to the Narrative Writing Checklist to see if you need to add anything to your writing.

Additional Narrative Writing Practice

Here is one to try on your own. Read this short story, "A Special Birthday Celebration," and respond to the writing task that follows. Do not forget to consider the format and the point of view, and use the box-and-bullets to help plan for your writing.

Note: This shorter passage is provided for additional writing practice only. Longer, comprehensive passages are provided at the end of this book in the practice test.

A Special Birthday Celebration

1 The big day is almost here. For the last six weeks, Sam has been keeping his room clean and doing all his chores. He even finished his homework every day before watching TV in the evening.

2 Sam is going to be nine years old on Saturday. He is having a special birthday celebration. The day will start with a special breakfast cooked by his grandmother. After breakfast, Sam will meet nine of his friends at the Pirate's Cove to play a round of miniature golf. Sam and his friends will finish the afternoon with a birthday lunch at their favorite pizza restaurant. Sam knows that he will have a great time with all of his friends, but he is waiting for the special surprise that his mom and dad have planned for the evening.

3 Sam has worked very hard for the last six weeks to show his parents that he can be responsible. His parents have said that they are very proud of him and that he has earned his special birthday celebration.

4 After his birthday dinner, Sam is going shopping with his mom and dad. They are going to Puppy Palace. Sam will get the puppy he has always wanted. The puppy is the best celebration!

Adapted from *New York State Grade 3 Elementary-Level English Language Arts Test*, by Jane A. Gallant (Barron's, 2008)

Narrative Writing Task

You have just read the story "A Special Birthday Celebration." Write your own story that continues where the passage ended. In your story, be sure to use what you have learned about the characters and the setting to tell what happens next.

Guidelines for Answering the Narrative Task

First, ask yourself what the format is that you will be using. Write the format on the line below.

Format for task: --

Next, ask yourself what point of view you will write from. What words will you use?

Point of view: --

Create a quick box-and-bullet plan for your writing.

-
-
-

Briefly outline what will happen in the next part of the story. Refer back to the charts in this chapter for additional support. In the bulleted section, jot down two to three sensory details or character descriptions, feelings, or reactions. Use this format to help guide your writing.

CHAPTER 3

Literary Analysis Task

Overview

The Literary Analysis Task is another PARCC writing task. You may also see it called LAT, which is short for Literary Analysis Task. In the LAT you will read two texts and compose an essay in which you discuss both readings. Both texts will have some things in common. One text will be short and the second text will be extended (or longer). You will need to read the story, answer the questions, and then complete a written essay that incorporates *both* texts into your response.

You will have Evidence-Based Selected-Response (EBSR) questions and Technology-Enhanced Constructed-Response (TECR) questions to answer. Review Chapter 2 for guidance on answering these types of questions.

You may be thinking that this sounds complicated. Well, just as with anything you do, the more you practice, the better you become!

Reading for Understanding

The most important thing you need to do during this assessment is to READ the text for understanding. Be an active reader!

You will need to use evidence from *both* texts. It might be helpful to have a piece of paper in front of you as you read each text. You can jot down important information as you read. The note-taking chart can look something like the chart below:

Text 1	Text 2
Key details:	Key details:

What Good Readers Do

Good readers think a lot when they read. This chart will help you understand the thinking that good readers use to help them understand the text they are reading.

Before you begin reading	• Think about the title. • If there are any illustrations, look at them closely. Think about what they show and how it will relate to the text. • Has the author included bold print headings to help you organize and understand the information? • Prepare to jot down some key details as you read each text.

During reading	• Notice the setting, theme, and order of events (plot). • Think about the characters' actions and feelings and how they change from the beginning to the end of the story. • Think about the story structure. Is there – a problem and solution? – cause and effect? – a sequence of events? • Think about the main idea and key details. • Question the text: – Do you understand how characters' actions contribute to the sequence of events? – Do you understand the central message, moral, or lesson in the text? – What are the character traits? – Do you understand the characters' feelings? • Draw conclusions and make inferences. – Sometimes an author does not write everything the reader needs to know in the text. Instead, the author includes enough information, or clues, for the reader to draw a conclusion about what is happening in the story. – The reader has to think along with the author and draw a logical conclusion about what the author really means. • Pay attention to the words the author uses: – If the words are new to you, use context clues to help you understand the meaning. – Does the author use words to help the reader create an image in the reader's mind? • Monitor your thinking: – If your mind stops thinking about the words you are reading, STOP, and read the section again. – If you find that you do not understand the text, go back and read it again.
After reading	• Read the question carefully. • Make sure you understand the question before you write your answer. • Look at the notes you jotted down for each text. Is there anything you need to add?

Understanding Types of Passages

Nonfiction		
Genre	**Features of the Genre**	**Strategies**
Informational text: Article	• It provides factual information. • Text is organized (text structure) to help readers understand the information. • It may contain graphic organizers such as photographs, charts, and diagrams to help the reader understand the topic. • Bold headings tell the reader the topic of each section in the text. • New vocabulary words are explained directly or through the use of context clues.	• Use the text structure to help you organize your thinking. • Read the headings carefully. • Use the information included in the graphic organizers. • Underline the important information and details as you read. • Take notes as you read. • Use the clues the author provides to learn the new words in the text.
Informational text: How-to	• Information is presented in the order it must occur. • Cue words include: first, second, third, next, last, finally.	• Follow the order presented in the text. • Do not leave out steps in the process when you recall information. • Look for cue words to follow the order of events. • Answer questions in the proper order of events.
Personal narratives	• The author is recalling an event that really happened. • The setting and characters are real. • The author's purpose is usually to share a memory with the reader. • The characters' feelings are important and often provide the reader with important information to help the reader understand and appreciate the author's memory	• Pay attention to the feelings expressed by the characters. • Pay attention to the characters' actions. • Highlight or take notes about the characters' feelings and learn if they change from the beginning to the end of the story.

Fiction		
Genre	**Features of the Genre**	**Strategies**
Fantasy	• It is a story that could never really happen. • Some or all of the characters are made up. • The setting may not be a real place. • Animals and imaginary characters may talk and communicate with realistic characters. • Time does not always pass in minutes, hours, and days.	• Pay special attention to the story elements: setting, characters, and time. • Highlight or take notes on the important elements. • As you read, try to visualize (picture) what is happening in the story.
Science fiction	• The main events might really happen, but something about them may not seem real.	• Look for the use of time travel or animals that talk. • Look for imaginary settings.
Fable	• It is a short tale that usually teaches a moral or a lesson. • Characters are often nonliving things or animals that talk and act like human beings.	• Look for animals that act like humans. • Pay attention to the story elements. • Focus on the conflict, the problem, and the solution. • Look for the lesson learned by one or more of the characters.
Realistic fiction	• The characters are fictional (not real), but the story is based on situations that could really happen. • The setting is often a place the reader knows or could recognize.	• Pay attention to the story elements. • Highlight or take notes about the setting, characters, and events.

Fiction (continued)		
Genre	**Features of the Genre**	**Strategies**
Folktale	• Plot is important. • There is often a lesson to be learned. • Folktales deal with ordinary people who do not have special powers. • A tall tale is a folktale that exaggerates details to help the reader understand the meaning of the tale.	• Pay attention to the plot and the lesson learned. • Highlight or take notes on important information. • Highlight or take notes on the lesson taught and learned at the end of the tale. • Highlight or take notes on the exaggerations the author uses to tell the tale.

Poetry		
Genre	**Features of the Genre**	**Strategies**
Poetry	• It is not always written in full and complete sentences. • The author's choice of words is important. • A great deal of meaning is provided in each line. • Figurative language is important. • Words are often used to create a sensory image for the reader. • Some poems use rhyme.	• Read the poem more than one time. • Look for the main idea or theme of the poem. • Focus your attention on the sensory imagery the writer is trying to present to the reader. • Focus on your thoughts and feelings as you read the poem again. • Highlight or take notes on the sensory images described by the author.

Understanding Story Elements

Story Elements	
Characters	The characters are who the story is about. Characters can be real or make-believe. They can also be animals or things. A story may have many characters, but a main character (or characters) are the most important characters in the story. When reading, think about: • What the character looks like • How the character acts and reacts to others • How a character changes
Setting	The setting is when and where the story takes place.
Problem	A story often has a problem that the characters are trying to overcome.
Solution	The solution is how the problem is resolved.
Theme	The theme is the main idea or meaning of the text. The theme of a story can also refer to a lesson or message the story is trying to tell us. Some stories have only one theme or message. Other stories have many lessons or messages.

Format for Response

Taking a close look!

Here is a possible Literary Analysis Task (LAT) question. The writing task is based on two stories, "The Girl and the Flute" and "The Quiltmaker's Gift." Think about how you would respond to the question. What are you being asked to do?

Sample Writing Task

"The Emperor's Gift" and "Lilly's Adventure" both try to teach important lessons to the characters in the stories. Write an essay that explains what lessons they taught and how the Emperor's and Lilly's words and actions are important to the plots of each of the stories. Use what you learned about the characters to support your essay.

Now, how do you begin? The most important thing you need to do is to make sure you read both stories. Also, jot down notes for both texts using a two-column chart. Think about what the question is asking you to do. The question states that in both stories the Emperor and Lilly try to teach lessons to the other characters in the stories. The question asks you to write about the lessons they tried to teach and to explain how each of the character's words and actions are important to the plot of the story.

Remember that the plot is the *action* in the story. It includes the problem and the solution.

Think about what the task is asking you to do. You may want to reread the task and look for a key word or words. Is the task asking you to do any of the following?

- ☑ Describe
- ☑ Compare/Contrast
- ☑ Explain
- ☑ Analyze

➔ **Bottom line:** *In the Literary Analysis Task you have to find similarities and/or differences in two texts.*

A good framework for literary analysis might look like this:

Paragraph 1 BOTH TEXTS	Introduction • Start with an opening statement/hook. • Mention the title of both texts that you read with a brief overview. Restate the question with emphasis on how both texts have some similarities and differences.
Paragraph 2 TEXT 1	Text 1 • Start this paragraph with an introductory statement about the first text. • Restate the key details of the text and what the question is asking you to examine (in this example, the important lesson learned, words and actions that are important to the story). Provide text evidence. Quote a few sentences that support what you are stating. You may also want to retell a part from the story in your own words.
Paragraph 3 TEXT 2	Text 2 • Start this paragraph with an introductory statement about the second text. • Restate the key details of the text (plot) and especially what the question is asking you to examine. Provide text evidence. Quote a few sentences that support what you are stating. You may also retell a part from the story in your own words.
Paragraph 4 BOTH TEXTS	Conclusion • This is where you have to discuss *both* texts and ways that they are similar and different. Remember to go back to the question and restate your response. • Make sure you have a closing statement.

Student Checklist

The literary analysis task will ask you to compare and contrast two pieces of literature. As you continue to practice, use this checklist to help you focus on important points. Remember, the more you practice, the better you will become!

Reading Comprehension What ideas about the text will I explain? What parts of the text will I use to respond?	☐ I figured out what to explain about the way the writer of the text wrote the text. ☐ I identified examples from the text to support the ideas I explained. ☐ I included specific details from the text to describe the parts of text that I used in my explanation. ☐ If the task asked me to write about two different texts, I figured out what was important to tell about each text.
Writing to Explain I organized my response to stay focused on important ideas. I included good examples.	☐ I organized an essay that explained the ideas I figured out based on the task. ☐ I wrote a clear introduction that told what I would explain in my essay. ☐ I focused each paragraph on one idea that is important to understanding how the writer organized the text. ☐ I included examples and details to support each point I made. ☐ I used linking words to connect ideas and parts. ☐ I wrote a clear conclusion.
Conventions My spelling and punctuation help keep my ideas clear.	☐ I capitalized the first word in a sentence and any proper noun. ☐ I used quotation marks if I included a quote. ☐ I spelled most words correctly.

Used with permission from *DePaul University Center for Urban Education*

Now you have a good idea of what you will need to know in order to write a great essay! Use the checklist and information in this chapter to help you. Remember, in this task you will need to read two texts, answer questions about what you have read, and then construct an essay that explores a certain aspect of the text. Let's practice with two shorter texts.

Let's Practice!

The purpose of this chapter is to provide practice with the writing tasks. Compared to what you will see on an actual test, the texts here are shorter and there are fewer questions. During the actual test, you will be given more TECR and EBSR questions and longer texts.

The practice tests at the end of this book will provide you with a full set of questions and more in-depth passages that provide a complete overview of the Literary Analysis Task expectations.

Remember, in this task you are allowed to go back to the story to help you!

Literary Analysis Task 1

Directions: Read the two fables below titled "The Crow and the Pitcher" and "The Clever Crow." As you read, think about the actions of the characters and the events of the fables. Answer the questions to help you write your essay.

Tip: Use a T-chart or the chart below to jot down details from each story as you read.

Text 1 "The Crow and the Pitcher"	Text 2 "The Clever Crow"

Text 1

The Crow and the Pitcher

Adapted from *Aesop's Fables*

1 A Crow, half-dead with thirst, came upon a pitcher which had once been full of water; but when the Crow put its beak into the mouth of the pitcher he found that only very little water was left in it. He knew he would not survive the day without a drop of water.

2 He **strived** to reach the water with all his might, but despite his best efforts he could not reach far enough down to get at it. He tried, and he tried, but at last had to give up in despair.

3 Then a brilliant thought came to him, and he took a pebble and dropped it into the pitcher. Then he took another pebble and dropped it into the pitcher. Then he took another pebble and dropped that into the pitcher. He continued to drop pebble by pebble into the pitcher.

4 At last, he saw the water rise up near him, and after casting in a few more pebbles he was able to quench his thirst and save his life.

1. **Part A.** What is the moral of "The Crow and the Pitcher"?

O A. Old friends are the best friends.
O B. It's better to be safe than sorry.
O C. Never give up!
O D. Honesty is the best policy.

Part B. What detail from the story provides the **best** evidence for the answer to Part A?

O A. The Crow was angry that he could not reach the water.
O B. The Crow placed pebble by pebble into the pitcher and finally reached the water.
O C. The Crow looked around for animals to help him.
O D. The Crow knew he could never reach the water.

2. **Part A.** Which statement best describes what the picture adds to the story?

O A. The picture shows that the Crow gave up.
O B. The picture shows that the Crow is lost.
O C. The picture shows that the Crow is trying to get to the water.
O D. The picture shows that the Crow does not have enough pebbles.

Part B. Which sentence from the story **best** supports the answer to Part A?

O A. "He continued to drop pebble by pebble into the pitcher." (paragraph 3)
O B. ". . . but despite his best efforts he could not reach far enough down to get at it." (paragraph 2)
O C. "A Crow, half-dead with thirst, came upon a pitcher . . ." (paragraph 1)
O D. "He knew he would not survive the day without a drop of water." (paragraph 1)

3. **Part A.** What does **strived** mean as it is used in paragraph 2 of "The Crow and the Pitcher"?

O A. lost
O B. tried
O C. cried
O D. excited

Part B. What statement best supports the answer to Part A?

O A. ". . . but despite his best efforts he could not reach far enough down to get at it." (paragraph 2)
O B. "Then a brilliant thought came to him . . ." (paragraph 3)
O C. "A Crow, half-dead with thirst, came upon a pitcher . . ." (paragraph 1)
O D. "At last, he saw the water rise up near him . . ." (paragraph 4)

Text 2

The Clever Crow

Adapted from a Panchatantra Tale

1 Once upon a time, there stood a huge banyan tree on the outskirts of a small village. In this tree there lived a crow with her young ones. One day, a snake came to live in the hole at the bottom of the tree. The crow was not happy at the arrival of the snake, but could do nothing.

2 After a few days, the female crow hatched a few more eggs and some more baby crows were born. When the crow went out in search of food, the snake crawled up the tree and ate up the babies. When the crow came back, she could not locate her babies. She searched high and low, but to no avail. The crow was full of grief on the sad loss of her young ones. Whenever the crow laid eggs, the snake would eat them up. The crow felt helpless. "That evil snake. I must do something. Let me go and talk to him," thought the crow.

3 The next morning, the crow went to the snake and said politely, "Please spare my eggs, dear friend. Let us live like good neighbors and not disturb each other."

4 "Huh! You cannot expect me to go hungry. Eggs are what I eat," replied the snake, in a nasty tone.

5 The crow felt furious—she could not believe the snake would be so cruel! She thought, "I must teach that snake a lesson."

6 The very next day, the crow was flying over the king's palace. She saw the princess wearing an expensive necklace. Suddenly a thought flashed in her mind and she swooped down, picked up the necklace in her beak, and flew off to her nest.

7 When the princess saw the crow flying off with her necklace, she screamed, "Somebody help! The crow has taken my necklace!"

8 Soon the palace guards were running around in search of the necklace. Within a short time the guards found the crow. She still sat with the necklace hanging from her beak.

9 The clever crow thought, "Now is the time to act." And she dropped the necklace, which fell right into the snake's pit.

10 As the guards were trying to take the necklace out with the help of a stick, the snake came out of the hole. "A snake! Kill it!" they shouted. With big sticks, they beat the snake and killed it. They then took the necklace and returned to their palace. The crow, from a distance, was happy to see the sight. The crow was relieved. "Now my eggs will be safe," she thought. From then on, she led a happy and peaceful life with her young ones in the banyan tree.

4. **Part A.** What does **furious** mean as it is used in paragraph 5 of "The Clever Crow"?

O A. scared
O B. angry
O C. worried
O D. excited

Part B. Which statement **best** supports the answer to Part A?

O A. ". . . she could not believe the snake would be so cruel!" (paragraph 5)
O B. "'Now my eggs will be safe,' she thought." (paragraph 10)
O C. "Please spare my eggs, dear friend." (paragraph 3)
O D. ". . . they beat the snake and killed it." (paragraph 10)

5. Tell what happens in "The Clever Crow." Select three of the **most important** details about the story from the sentences below. Write them in the correct order using the graphic organizer.

The snake is killed and the eggs are safe.
The snake eats the crow's eggs.
The crow wants to be friends with the snake.
The crow drops the princess's necklace into the snake's pit.
The snake lives in the forest.

Key Details

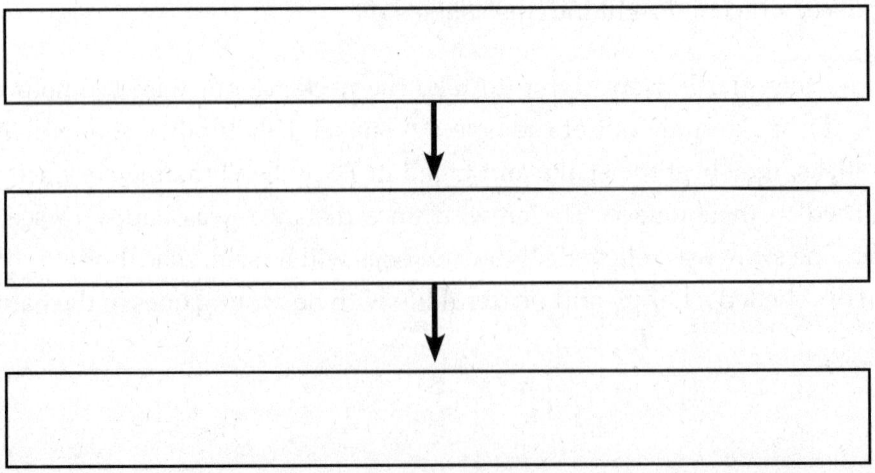

6. From the box below, select a character trait that describes the crow and a character trait that describes the snake. Then, from the list given, select a supporting detail that provides evidence for the trait you selected.

Possible Character Traits	Possible Supporting Details
Smart	She took the necklace and dropped it into the pit.
Lazy	He lived in a hole in the bottom of the tree.
Mean	She lived in a banyan tree.
Fun	The snake continued to eat the eggs.

	Crow	Snake
Character Trait		
Supporting Detail		

Answers

"The Crow and the Pitcher"

1. The correct answer for Part A is choice C, "Never give up!" The Crow did not give up on trying to get water from the pitcher.

   The correct answer for Part B is choice B. "The Crow placed pebble by pebble into the pitcher and finally reached the water." This shows that the Crow never gave up even though he had to place one pebble at a time in the pitcher to get the water to rise.

2. The correct answer for Part A is choice C, "The picture shows that the Crow is trying to get to the water." The picture shows the crow picking up the pebble in his beak and placing it in the pitcher.

   The correct answer for Part B is choice A, "He continued to drop pebble by pebble into the pitcher."

3. The correct answer for Part A is choice B, "tried." In paragraph 2 it says, "He **strived** to reach the water with all his might, but despite his best efforts he

could not reach far enough down to get at it." When you come to a vocabulary question, sometimes it is helpful to try to replace the word in the sentence and see if it makes sense. We could say "The Crow tried to reach the water but could not." This would make sense in the context of the paragraph.

The correct answer for Part B is choice A. ". . . but despite his best efforts he could not reach far enough down to get at it." When this sentence states "despite his best efforts," it shows that the Crow was trying.

"The Clever Crow"

4. The correct answer for Part A is choice B angry. The crow was angry that the snake did not want to stop eating the eggs.

   The correct answer for Part B is choice A, ". . . she could not believe the snake would be so cruel!" This answer supports that the crow was furious or angry at the snake.

5. The correct order of events is:

   The snake eats the crow's eggs.

   The crow drops the princess's necklace into the snake's pit.

   The snake is killed and the eggs are safe.

   These events are the main events that happen in the story. Often, main events (the plot) focus on a problem, what is being done to solve that problem, and how the story ends.

6.

	Crow	Snake
Character Trait	Smart	Mean
Supporting Detail	She took the necklace and dropped it into the pit.	The snake continued to eat the eggs.

The crow was smart when she figured out a way to solve the problem of the snake eating her eggs. The supporting detail, "She took the necklace and dropped it into the pit" shows evidence that she was smart.

The snake was mean because he did not care that the crow wanted him to stop eating the eggs. The supporting detail "The snake continued to eat the eggs" supports that he was mean.

Literary Analysis Task 2

Directions: In both "The Crow and the Pitcher" and "The Clever Crow," the main characters find a clever solution to a problem. Write an essay that explains how the words and actions of both crows are important to the plots of the stories. Use what you learned about the characters to support your essay. Be sure to use specific details from each story to support your ideas.

Helpful Hints:

- Reread the question and make sure you understand what it is asking you to do. In this task you are asked to explain how the words and the actions of the crow contribute to the plot.
- Remember, the plot refers to the problem and the solution.
- Since you are asked to include words and actions, it might be a good idea to put a quote from the main character or to find a sentence that shows action.
- Remember, you will need to use text evidence as you describe *both* stories.
- Use the format chart found in the chapter to help guide your writing.
- Do not forget to use transition words to give your writing some organization. Use words such as *first, next, then, after that,* and *finally* in your paragraphs. In your fourth paragraph you will mention both texts and may want to use words such as *similar, even though, different, differ, however, but, in conclusion.*
- Do not make your writing sound flat. Add some excitement into your writing. Do not just list facts from the story, but try to add some descriptive words!

Sample Response

Paragraph 1 Both texts Introduction • Opening statement/hook • Mention the title of both stories that you read with a brief overview. • Restate the question with emphasis on how both stories have some similarities and differences.	Aesop's Fables are great stories that teach morals or lessons. The stories "The Crow and the Pitcher" and "The Clever Crow" are great examples of how characters can solve tricky problems. Even though there are crows in both stories, they have very different problems that need to be solved. Through hard work and being clever they both are able to solve their problems!
Paragraph 2 Text 1 • Introductory statement about the first text • Restate the key details of the text (plot), and what the question is wanting you to examine (in this example, the important lesson learned, words and actions that are important to the plot). • Provide text evidence. Lift a quote or a few sentences that support what you are stating.	The first story, "The Crow and the Pitcher" starts out with the Crow being very thirsty. He was lucky to find a pitcher with water in it, but unlucky too because the neck of the pitcher was too narrow. The Crow could not reach the water. The story states, "The poor thing felt as if he must die of thirst." Next, the Crow had a great idea! He decided to drop pebbles into the pitcher until the water rose. This was a smart idea because now he could drink the water—problem solved!

Paragraph 3 Text 2 • Introductory statement about the second text • Restate the key details of the text (plot) and especially what the question is asking you to examine (in this example, the important lesson learned, words and actions that are important to the plot). • Provide text evidence. Lift a quote or a few sentences that support what you are stating.	The second story, "The Clever Crow" had a very different problem. The snake kept eating the crow's eggs. The crow did try to talk things out when she said, "Please spare my eggs, dear friend. Let us live like good neighbors and not disturb each other." But the snake was doing what snakes tend to do—and continued to eat the eggs! That all ended when the crow played a trick on the snake and dropped a necklace from the king's palace into the snake pit! When the guards found the necklace they killed the snake. The crow was happy and said, "Now my eggs will be safe!"
Paragraph 4 Both texts Conclusion • This is where you have to discuss BOTH texts and how they are similar and different. (In this example you would discuss the differences and similarities in the lessons they learned and how the words and actions are important to the plots of the stories.) Closing statement	To sum things up, the characters in both stories found clever solutions to their problems. The first character solved the problem of being thirsty and the second character solved the problem of saving her eggs from the snake. It goes to show that smart thinking can really help you when you are in trouble! Also, in both stories the crows never gave up hope. So, the next time you are faced with a tricky problem, remember these fables and try to find a creative solution!

Research Simulation Task

CHAPTER 4

Overview

Have you ever had to do a research project for your teacher? Think about what steps you needed to take to complete it. You most likely had to research more than one source. A source can be a book, magazine, online website, video, chart, or any other thing that provides you with the information on the topic you are researching. This task is going to ask you to look at some sources. The good news is that the sources will be provided for you! After you read, listen, or view the information, you will answer a few questions. When you have finished looking at the two sources, you will be asked to write an essay.

You will need to combine information from BOTH sources into your written response. You will also need to provide several quotes or excerpts to support your essay. You may have heard the expression "text evidence." Text evidence means going back to the text and using evidence or examples from the text to support your answer. Well, you will need to provide some text evidence in your response. You can go back to the sources to get information. Sometimes it is useful to jot things down as you read. If you are taking the test on a computer, you will be able to highlight important words, phrases, or sentences.

Understanding Informational and Explanatory Writing

This type of writing involves giving information to the reader about a topic by sequencing, comparing and contrasting, reporting, describing, or explaining. It conveys information and attempts to increase the reader's knowledge on the subject. Writers use the sources that they are given and use examples, facts, and details.

Format for Response

The structure of the essay is usually the following.

Introductory Paragraph	Provide a clear opening statement in the first paragraph of the essay. This opening statement should restate the question in sentence form. Get the attention of the reader with a "hook." • Ask a question such as "Have you ever wondered?" or "Did you know . . . ?" • Use a quote from the text. • State your topic clearly and avoid using "I," if possible. • Briefly state the main points. • Save facts and examples for the detail paragraphs (body).
Transitional Words	Use transitional words and phrases between the introduction, body, and conclusion. Some examples of transitional words in expository and informational texts are: *for example, in addition, also, in fact, for this reason, however, although, first, second, last, in conclusion, in summary.*
Body If you want someone to believe it, you must support it!	The Body paragraphs **must** include evidence from the text to support what you are writing. Try to give two to three facts from the texts if you can. Don't just list the facts, but rather explain why each piece of evidence is important. Provide supporting details on each piece of evidence. Explain the idea. • Give reasons. • Provide facts/evidence. • Use an example from the text. • Use transition words. • Keep your reader interested!
Conclusion	The conclusion ties all the information together. Think about how you answered the question and the evidence you provided. • Summarize your main idea (provide support). • Restate your topic in different words. Ways to end your essay: • Challenge your readers. • Focus on the future. • Pose a question.

Helpful Tips

When you take the test you will be able to have scrap paper. This will be a great tool to help you jot down ideas as you read through the text. You can make a simple T-chart and bullet important information as you read. This will help you with the questions and with the writing task. You may want to highlight important facts so you can use them in your essay. Remember that the T-chart is for your eyes only! It will not be counted in the scoring of your task, but it will be useful to refer to when you need to answer questions.

Text 1	Text 2

Student Checklist

The research simulation task will ask you to write about two different texts. They may be about the same topic or idea. Use this checklist as you continue to practice writing responses to research simulation tasks.

Reading Comprehension What are the important ideas in each text? What information supports them?	☐ I figured out what the important ideas in each text are. ☐ I identified information that supports the ideas in each text. ☐ I used those ideas and facts in my response to the task. ☐ If the task asked me to combine information, then I chose the most important information from each source to use. ☐ If the task asked me to compare information from two texts, I identified the ideas and information that are alike in the texts. ☐ If the task asked me to contrast two texts, I identified ideas and information that are different between them.
Writing to Explain I organized my response to stay focused on important ideas and information. I included good examples.	☐ I organized an essay that responds to the task. ☐ I wrote a clear introduction that told what I would explain in my essay. ☐ I focused each paragraph on one part of my response. ☐ I included examples and details to support each point I made. ☐ I used linking words to connect ideas and parts. ☐ I wrote a clear conclusion.

Conventions My spelling and punctuation help keep my ideas clear.	☐ I capitalized the first word in a sentence and any proper noun. ☐ I used quotation marks if I included a quote. ☐ I spelled most words correctly.

Used with permission from *DePaul University Center for Urban Education*

Now that you have an overview of the requirements for the Research Simulation Task, you will practice with two texts. Just as with the Narrative Writing and Literary Analysis tasks, you will have questions to answer after each text. After you have read *both* texts, you will be asked to write an essay. Remember to use text evidence from *both* sources in your essay. Okay, let's try it!

Let's Practice!

The purpose of this chapter is to provide practice with the writing tasks, so the texts have been kept short and only a couple of questions have been provided. During the actual test you will be given more TECR and EBSR questions and longer texts.

The practice tests at the end of this book will provide you with a full set of questions and more in-depth passages that provide a complete overview of the Research Simulation Task expectations.

Remember, in this task you are allowed to go back into the story to help you!

Research Simulation

Directions: The two texts below discuss ways that germs are spread and what to do if you get the flu. As you read these texts, you will gather information and answer questions about how to prevent the spread of germs and what to do if you become sick. This will help you write an essay about the topic.

Read "The Buzz on Scuzz" and "Should You Go to School?" and answer the questions that follow.

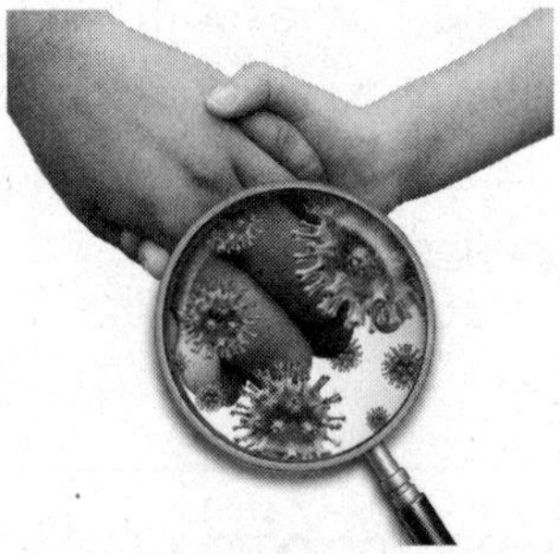

THE BUZZ ON SCUZZ!

1 They're so small you can't even see them. They multiply faster than the clothes that keep piling up on your floor. They're everywhere—they lurk in the water you drink, the food you eat, and the air you breathe. At this very moment they are in your stomach and on your skin. What's more, they've been around forever.

2 Sound like creatures from a horror movie? Nope! They are germs or, more scientifically, microbes. And there is more than one kind of microbe out there. Viruses, bacteria, fungi, and protozoa all qualify. Some of them can make you really sick if you're not careful.

3 Not to worry! Most germs/microbes are harmless, and some even help to keep you healthy. But some can make you very sick. Every day you come in contact with hidden germs, pretty much everywhere you go. Some of their favorite hangouts are bathrooms, kitchens, the cafeteria, the gym, and the locker room. And those are just the **obvious** places you would expect to find germs. Some places are not so obvious and you would never think germs hide

there! They also hide on pencils (remember when you chewed on it?), remote controls or game controllers (like the one you sneezed on last week), phones, pet cages, computer keyboards, stair railings, and doorknobs—pretty much anything your hands can touch.

4 Germs can spread when people touch things that are covered with them (like the door handle in a public restroom). These germs get on your hand and spread to other parts of your body when you touch your eyes, ears, or mouth! And they don't stop there—you spread germs when you touch something or someone else. But there is one thing you can do to stop germs in their tracks. **WASH YOUR HANDS!** Believe it or not, washing your hands is the **single most important thing you can do** to keep from getting sick or spreading your germs to others.

Source: *http://www.cdc.gov/bam/body/buzz-scuzz.html*

1. Part A. What is the meaning of **obvious** as it is used in paragraph 3?

O A. strange
O B. known
O C. cold
O D. dark

Part B. What detail from the story **best** supports your answer to Part A?

O A. ". . . you would expect to find germs." (paragraph 3)
O B. " Most germs/microbes are harmless . . ." (paragraph 3)
O C. ". . . you spread germs when you touch something or someone else." (paragraph 4)
O D. ". . . some even help to keep you healthy." (paragraph 3)

2. **Part A.** According to the article, how do germs spread?

- O A. when you go out in the cold
- O B. when you skip meals
- O C. when you touch something
- O D. when you have a fever

Part B. Which detail from the story **best** supports your answer to Part A?

- O A. "Every day you come in contact with hidden germs, pretty much everywhere you go." (paragraph 3)
- O B. "They multiply faster than the clothes that keep piling up on your floor." (paragraph 1)
- O C. "Germs can spread when people touch things that are covered with them . . ." (paragraph 4)
- O D. "Believe it or not, washing your hands is the **single most important thing you can do** to keep from getting sick or spreading your germs to others." (paragraph 4)

3. Select and write in the boxes below, three details that best support the main idea, "Germs can be spread in many ways."

Possible Supporting Details

A. Germs spread when people touch things that are covered with them.

B. Washing your hands prevents germs from spreading.

C. You spread germs when you touch something or someone else.

D. Not all germs are bad.

E. Germs get on your hand and spread to other parts of your body when you touch your eyes, ears, or mouth.

MAIN IDEA
Germs Can Be Spread in Many Ways

Supporting Detail 1	**Supporting Detail 2**	**Supporting Detail 3**

Should You Go to School?

1 Have you ever gone to school when you didn't feel so well? Everyone has probably done it, but if you think you have the flu, it's very important to stay home from school.

2 Here's why: influenza flu is an illness that could make some people very sick. So we want to do our best to keep it from spreading around. The flu is contagious; if you have the flu, you can spread it easily.

3 Symptoms of the flu are a fever plus one or more of these:

- cough
- sore throat
- runny nose
- body aches
- headaches
- tiredness

4 Some people with the flu also might have diarrhea or vomiting. If you have flu-like symptoms, home is where you should be.

5 By staying home from school (and away from crowds in general), you make it less likely that you will make other people sick. And if it turns out you do have the flu, rest at home is what you need to get better.

What to Do

6 Take these steps if you feel sick:

✔ Tell your mom or dad, so they can check you out. They might want to call your doctor to talk about whether you have the flu or some other sickness.

✔ Stay home from school and other crowded places. Also, try not to make other people in your family sick. Do that by washing your hands often, coughing and sneezing into a tissue or your elbow—not into your hands!—and keeping your distance.

✔ Get rest, drink plenty of fluids, and feel better fast. Be sure to tell your mom or dad how you're feeling so they can take good care of you.

✔ Return to school only when you're feeling better, no longer coughing/ sneezing, and you haven't had a fever for at least 24 hours.

Source: *http://kidshealth.org/kid/h1n1_center/h1n1_school.html?tracking=K_RelatedArticle*

4. **Part A.** What is the meaning of the word **contagious** as it is used in paragraph 1?

O A. It makes you sneeze.
O B. You get a fever.
O C. You can pass it on to others.
O D. You need to see a doctor.

Part B. Which detail from the story supports your answer to Part A?

O A. "If you have flu-like symptoms, home is where you should be." (paragraph 4)
O B. ". . . if you have the flu you can spread it easily." (paragraph 2)
O C. "Some people with the flu also might have diarrhea or vomiting." (paragraph 4)
O D. ". . . influenza flu is an illness that could make some people very sick." (paragraph 2)

5. **Part A.** What is the main idea of the article, "Should You Go to School?"

O A. You need to get enough sleep at night.
O B. When you are sick you should see a doctor.
O C. You should stay home if you have the flu.
O D. When you get the flu you may need medicine.

Part B. Which detail from the article best supports your answer to Part A?

O A. "Some people with the flu also might have diarrhea or vomiting." (paragraph 4)
O B. "By staying home from school (and away from crowds in general), you make it less likely that you will make other people sick." (paragraph 5)
O C. "Tell your mom or dad, so they can check you out. They may want to call your doctor to talk about whether you have the flu or some other sickness." (paragraph 6)
O D. "Symptoms of the flu are a fever plus one or more of these . . ." (paragraph 3)

6. Complete the chart below by using words from the box to describe symptoms of the flu.

Fever
Itchy skin
Runny nose
Bleeding
Vomiting
Coughing

Symptoms of the Flu

Research Simulation Writing Task:

You have read two texts, "The Buzz on Scuzz" and "Should You Go to School?" Both texts give information about getting sick. Think about the ways the authors provide information on the topics. Write an essay that helps students know how germs are spread and what to do if they get the flu. Remember to use details from both articles to support your ideas.

Answers

1. **Part A.** The correct answer is choice B, "known." The sentence before the word **obvious** mentions bathrooms, kitchens, the cafeteria, the gym, and the locker room. The article does not refer to them as strange, cold, or dark, but they are places that are known to you.

   Part B. The correct answer for Part B is choice A, ". . . you would expect to find germs." This sentence supports Part A that **obvious** means places that are known to you. When answering vocabulary questions, you must go back and reread the sentences before and after the word to see if there are any context clues to help you figure out the meaning.

2. **Part A.** The correct answer is choice C, "When you touch something." This choice best answers the question on how germs are spread.

   Part B. The correct answer is choice C, "Germs can spread when people touch things that are covered with them." This answer choice best supports how germs are spread. Remember not to select an answer just because it sounds familiar. Most of the sentences given as answer choices are found in the article, but only *one* will be the *best* choice.

3. The correct answers for question 3 are **A**, **C**, and **E**. These details best support the main idea, "Germs can be spread in many ways."

   Possible Supporting Details

   A. *Germs spread when people touch things that are covered with them.*

      This answer **correctly** supports how germs are spread. When people touch things that are covered with germs, the germs can spread.

   B. *Washing your hands prevents germs from spreading.*

      This is an **incorrect choice**. This statement tells you how to *prevent* germs from spreading. The question is asking for details to support ways that germs *can* spread.

   C. *You spread germs when you touch something or someone else.*

      This answer **correctly** supports how germs are spread. When you touch something or someone else you can spread germs.

D. Not all germs are bad.

This is an **incorrect choice**. This sentence is telling you that not all germs are bad, but it is not a supporting detail on how germs are spread.

E. Germs get on your hand and spread to other parts of your body when you touch your eyes, ears, or mouth.

This answer **correctly** supports how germs are spread. When germs get on your hands, they spread when you touch your eyes, ears, or mouth.

4. **Part A**. The correct answer is choice C, "You can pass it on to others." The other answer choices do not support the clues that are in paragraph 1 for the word **contagious**. When you get to a vocabulary word, make sure you read the sentences that come before and after the word. Often, reading the word with the surrounding sentences helps you to determine the meaning.

   Part B. The correct answer is choice B, ". . . if you have the flu you can spread it easily." This sentence *best* supports the answer "You can pass it on to others."

5. **Part A**. The correct answer is choice C, "You should stay home if you have the flu." In this story, the title gives you a clue to the main idea. Sometimes the title can help, but not always. Do not get tricked by answer choices that you may know to be true for yourself. For example, you may believe that you need a good night's sleep, that when you are sick you should see a doctor, and that you may need medicine, but the main idea of the entire article is "You should stay at home if you have the flu."

   Part B. The correct answer is choice B, "By staying home from school (and away from crowds in general), you make it less likely that you will make other people sick." This supports the main idea in Part A about staying home when you have the flu. It is always a good idea to check your answers for Part A and Part B to make sure they makes sense and that your choice for Part B is the best supporting statement for your answer to Part A.

6.

Symptoms of the Flu

Fever
Runny nose
Vomiting
Coughing

These are the symptoms of the flu as described in the article. Bleeding and itching are not mentioned as symptoms. Sometimes it is helpful to go back and highlight the different details as you reread.

Sample Response for the Research Simulation Writing Task

Have you ever gotten the flu? It is not fun and can really make you feel sick! Did you know there are ways to prevent the spread of germs and things you can do to avoid getting sick in the first place? Also, if you should happen to get sick, there are a few important things you will need to know. "The Buzz on Scuzz" and "Should I Go to School?" are two texts that give important information about being sick. If you want to prevent getting sick or want to know what to do when you are sick, pay attention!

The first text, "The Buzz on Scuzz," tells important ways to prevent the spread of germs. Did you know that germs are everywhere? The text says, "They're everywhere—they lurk in the water you drink, the food you eat, and the air you breathe. At this very moment they are in your stomach and on your skin." Since they are everywhere, it is really easy to pick up germs and get sick. There is a simple solution to help stop the spread of germs. The end of the article says, "Believe it or not, washing your hands is the single most important thing you can do to keep from getting sick or spreading your germs to others." To sum it up, even though germs are found everywhere, you can wash your hands often to make sure you do not get sick. What happens if you do get sick?

If you still managed to get sick, what should you do? The second article, "Should You Go to School?" tells us not to go to school if we are sick. It states, "By staying home from school (and away from crowds in general), you make it less likely that you will make other people sick. And if it turns out you do have the flu, rest at home is what you need to get better." The key to feeling better and stopping the spread of germs is to stay home, rest up, and drink plenty of fluids. Return to school only if you are feeling better and haven't had a fever in 24 hours.

Finally, both articles discuss the importance of washing your hands. The first text wants you to wash your hands to help prevent you from getting germs that may get you sick. The second text wants you to wash your hands if you are sick. This way you will prevent someone else from getting sick. A final reminder is, "Return to school only when you're feeling better, no longer coughing/sneezing, and you haven't had a fever for at least 24 hours." Finally, if we all do our part, we can help to stop germs from spreading and we can stay healthy!

Taking a Computerized Test

CHAPTER 5

Overview

Taking a test on the computer may be new to you. It is important that you understand how to work with certain tools on the computer, such as the following:

- Back/forward arrow
- Review button
- Pointer tool
- Notepad
- Answer eliminator
- Text highlight
- Line reader
- Zoom/Magnification
- Scrollbar
- Drag and drop

You will also need to become familiar with the tabs at the top of each article or story. The tabs allow you to switch back and forth between two texts. Also, the box in which you write your story will enlarge as you continue to write. Don't be fooled into thinking that you need to write only a sentence or two!

Use the website below to become familiar with the different tools that you will need to know how to use during the PARCC test. It is important that you are able to easily navigate through the assessment. You do not want to waste time trying to figure out where the back arrow is or how to access both texts using the tab. You will not be fully prepared until you take this online tutorial:

http://parcc.pearson.com/tutorial/

Helpful Tips

Keyboarding

You will need to know how to use the keyboard and how the keys are laid out. The best way to become familiar with the keyboarding is to practice—A LOT! Try to practice typing for at least 15 minutes a day. The more you practice, the better prepared you will be!

Basic Computer Skills

You will need to know how to drag-and-drop and use other keyboarding skills with speed and accuracy. You also need to know how to operate the highlighting tool. You may also be required to watch a video and you should know how to turn it on, pause, and so on. Ideally, it would be best to practice on the same device that you will take the PARCC on, but if that is not possible, any computer will help sharpen your skills! Becoming comfortable with technology takes time and practice.

Stamina

You will be expected to read more than one text, answer questions, and write a response. This will require a lot of stamina on your part. You should read and type a little each day so that you are prepared for the tasks.

Also, the night before the test, make sure you get a proper night's sleep and eat a healthy breakfast. This will help to keep you focused.

Note Taking

You will be allowed to have paper and a pencil. Take notes as you read the text. They do not have to be long, detailed notes, but some bulleted notes will help you remember what you read. You may also want to number the paragraph that you are referring to.

Practice

You will want to practice writing stories on the computer. This will help you with your keyboarding skills. Remember, you will need to complete three writing tasks online. Try typing your essay/story to the practice tests. Remember, the more you practice, the better you will become!

Practice Test

IMPORTANT NOTE: Barron's has made every effort to create sample tests that accurately reflect the PARCC Assessment. However, the tests are constantly changing. The following two tests differ in length and content, but each will still provide a strong framework for third-grade students preparing for the assessment. Be sure to consult *http://www.parcconline.org* for all the latest testing information.

You will now take a practice test to prepare you for the PARCC Performance-Based Assessments. Remember to use the strategies that were mentioned in this book to help you.

Timing and Scoring

For planning purposes, use the suggested times given below.

Narrative Writing Task: 75 minutes
Literary Analysis Task: 90 minutes
Research Simulation Task: 90 minutes

Scoring EBSR and TECR Questions

Evidence-Based Selected-Response (two-part questions)

2 points if BOTH Part A and Part B are correct
1 point if Part A is correct and Part B is incorrect
0 points if Part A is incorrect, even if Part B is correct

Technology-Enhanced Constructed-Response

2 points if correct
1 point if partially correct
0 points if incorrect

Scoring the Prose Constructed-Response Questions

A PCR rubric, found in the appendix, will help you to score the writing tasks.

PERFORMANCE-BASED ASSESSMENT

Directions: Read each passage that follows and all the questions carefully. Some questions will ask you to choose one correct answer, while others will ask you to choose more than one correct answer. You may look back at the passage or passages as often as needed.

Some questions will ask you to provide a written response to the passages you have read. You may plan your response using scratch paper. Be sure to write your response on the lined paper provided in this book.

If you do not know the answer to a question, you may skip it and go on. If you finish the test early, you may review your answers and any questions you may have skipped.

Narrative Writing Task

Directions: Read the following story, "The Mermaids." As you read, pay close attention to the actions of the characters and the events in the story. Answer the questions that follow to help you prepare to write the narrative story.

The Mermaids

Adapted from a story by Sara Meehl

1 There once was a girl named Maggie who lived near the ocean. Every day, she would go outside, sit on the beach, and watch the waves roll in and out. One day, something in the waves caught her eye.

2 She heard laughter, splashing, and talking coming from the ocean. It sounded very near. Maggie looked around to be sure it wasn't her sister playing a trick on her. But her sister was not there. She looked at the waves again and saw a fin splash out of the water. It looked too big to belong to one of the fish that swam in the shallow water near the beach. Then, suddenly, two heads came into view.

3 "Hello," said one of the creatures. "I am Olivia, and this is Loretta. What is your name?"

4 "W-what," said Maggie, confused. "W-who are you? W-what are you doing in the water?"

5 "We are mermaids, of course!" said Loretta cheerfully.

6 "Really? I have never seen one before. Why are you at my house?" Maggie was very excited. Was she really talking to mermaids?

7 "My sister and I were just taking a swim and we saw you on the beach. We have never met a real girl before. You looked friendly so we thought we would say hello," said Olivia.

8 "Would you like to swim with us for a while?" asked Loretta.

9 "Yes, I would love that," said Maggie.

10 Maggie swam with her new mermaid friends until they heard a roaring sound coming from beneath the waves.

11 "That is our school bell," said Olivia. "We must go to school now. We will come back tomorrow if you would like to swim again."

12 "Yes. That would be great!" said Maggie. "See you tomorrow." Maggie could not wait to get home and tell her sister about her two new friends.

13 Maggie's sister did not believe her story. "There are no mermaids," she told Maggie. "You fell asleep in the hot sun and had a dream."

14 Maggie was upset. "That is not true. Come with me tomorrow and I will introduce you to my new friends."

15 The next day Maggie and her sister went to the beach and waited for Olivia and Loretta. Maggie's sister brought a camera and had it hanging from a strap on her neck. She did not believe Maggie. But, if the story was true, she was going to take a picture to show everyone that mermaids really do exist.

16 Maggie and her sister waited until it was almost dark. Their parents insisted that they come in for dinner. Maggie was disappointed that her friends had not come. Maggie's sister just laughed and said, "Sweet dreams," as she walked past Maggie and went inside for dinner.

17 As Maggie started to walk away she heard a voice that sounded like Olivia. It was Olivia!

18 "Where were you? I brought my sister here to meet you. Now she does not believe that you are real," said Maggie.

19 "We know. We saw her. We saw that she had a camera," said Loretta.

20 "That is why we could not come back to see you. The king of our land has warned us never to let humans see that we exist. Our king believes our lives would be different if people knew we really existed," said Olivia.

21 "We took a chance when we said hello to you. But we trust that you will keep us a secret," said Loretta.

22 "I understand," said Maggie. "Can we still be friends? I promise I will not tell anyone about you."

23 "Yes," said Olivia and Loretta at the same time. "Come back tomorrow and we will swim together again."

1. **Part A.** What caused the splashing that Maggie heard in paragraph 2 of this story?

O A. Some people were fishing in the water.
O B. A few dolphins were swimming close by.
O C. Two mermaids were playing in the water.
O D. Maggie's sister was swimming in the water.

Part B. What detail from the story **best** supports your answer to Part A?

O A. "Then, suddenly, two heads came into view." (paragraph 2)
O B. "But her sister was not there." (paragraph 2)
O C. "You fell asleep in the hot sun and had a dream." (paragraph 13)
O D. "Every day, she would go outside, sit on the beach, and watch the waves roll in and out." (paragraph 1)

2. **Part A.** Read this sentence from paragraph 1 of the story.

One day, something in the waves caught her eye.

The phrase **caught her eye** most likely means

O A. Something got into her eye.
O B. Someone touched her face.
O C. Something fell into the ocean.
O D. She noticed something in the ocean.

Part B. Which detail **best** helps to show what **caught her eye** means in the story?

O A. "Every day, she would go outside, sit on the beach, and watch the waves roll in and out." (paragraph 1)
O B. "Maggie's sister brought a camera and had it hanging from a strap on her neck." (paragraph 15)
O C. "She heard laughter, splashing, and talking coming from the ocean." (paragraph 2)
O D. "Maggie was disappointed that her friends had not come." (paragraph 16)

3. Part A. When Maggie saw the mermaids, she was **most likely** surprised because:

- O A. Maggie did not know where she was.
- O B. Maggie had never seen a mermaid before.
- O C. Maggie's parents were calling her.
- O D. Maggie saw her sister.

Part B. Which detail **best** supports your answer to Part A?

- O A. "Was she really talking to mermaids?" (paragraph 6)
- O B. "That is our school bell." (paragraph 11)
- O C. ". . . they heard a roaring sound coming from beneath the waves." (paragraph 10)
- O D. "As Maggie started to walk away she heard a voice that sounded like Olivia." (paragraph 17)

4. Part A. Why did Olivia and Loretta stay away from Maggie when she brought her sister to meet them?

- O A. The mermaids did not like Maggie's sister.
- O B. The mermaids had to go to school.
- O C. Maggie's sister had a camera to take a picture of the mermaids.
- O D. They wanted to play with their other friends.

Part B: Which **two** phrases from the story **best** support your answer?

- ☐ A. "We must go to school now. We will come back tomorrow if you would like to swim again." (paragraph 11)
- ☐ B. "That is not true. Come with me tomorrow and I will introduce you to my new friends." (paragraph 14)
- ☐ C. "You fell asleep in the hot sun and had a dream." (paragraph 13)
- ☐ D. "The king of our land has warned us never to let humans see that we exist." (paragraph 20)
- ☐ E. "Come back tomorrow and we will swim together again." (paragraph 23)
- ☐ F. "But, if the story was true, she was going to take a picture to show everyone that mermaids really do exist." (paragraph 15)

5. Complete the chart using details from the story. Write the details in the order in which they happened in the story.

Details:

Maggie promises not to tell anyone that the mermaids are real.

Maggie meets two mermaids at the beach.

The mermaids do not show up when Maggie's sister comes to see them.

Maggie tells her sister about the mermaids.

What Happens in the Story?

In the beginning,
Next,
Then,
At the end,

6. Pretending that you are Maggie, write a journal entry about an adventure she has with her new mermaid friends. Use details from the story to think about what Maggie is like. As you write your journal entry, be sure to include Maggie's thoughts and feelings about her new adventure. Also include information about how the other characters act.

Literary Analysis Task

Directions: Read the two stories below titled "The North Wind and the Sun" and "The Three Brothers." Both stories are folktales from different countries. Each story contains a moral that teaches a lesson. As you read, think about the actions of the characters and the events of the stories. Answer the questions to help you write an essay.

The North Wind and the Sun

Adapted from Aesop Fables

1 Long ago, the North Wind lived behind a high mountain. He knew that he was indeed the strongest and most powerful force in nature. He felt quite content having all this strength. Every now and again, he would show his strength in great, fierce wind storms that would cause all in his way to rush for safe shelter.

2 On the other side of the mountain lived the Sun. Unlike the North Wind, the Sun was quiet and gentle, but when given the opportunity, could be just as powerful as the North Wind.

3 One day, the boastful Wind announced to the Sun, "You know that I am the strongest and most powerful of all the weather!"

4 And the Sun replied, "All weather can be strong and powerful." The North Wind paid no reply to the Sun.

5 The North Wind continued to **boast** of great strength. He would brag to everyone he met about his great power and strength. The Sun, however, continued to protest this claim and argued that there was power in gentleness. But the North Wind did not understand how something could be both strong and gentle.

6 The relentless Wind continued to disagree. "All weather may be strong," said the North Wind, "but I am the strongest of all." The Sun announced, "I see a way to end our dispute. We shall have a contest. The weather that makes people remove most of their clothing will show that they are indeed the strongest of all."

7 The North Wind laughed at the Sun's challenge, but agreed to end this dispute once and for all.

8 At that time a man was traveling along a winding road. He was wearing a long, warm winter coat. "As a test of strength," said the Sun, "let us see which of us can take the coat off that man. You begin."

9 The North Wind laughed at the Sun's request. Surely, this would be a simple challenge.

10 The Sun rested behind a cloud and watched the North Wind at work.

11 "It will be quite simple for me to force the man to remove his coat," boasted the North Wind.

12 The North Wind rose from the sky and swirled around. Then, with a powerful blow he forced a mighty push of wind in the direction of the man traveling down the road. It blew so hard that birds clung to the trees. The world was whirling with dust and leaves. Massive gale winds swept across the land, but the harder the North Wind blew, the tighter the shivering man clung to his coat. The North Wind continued to blow, but it was useless. The man continued to clench his coat tighter. The North Wind finally ceased and gave up.

13 "This is impossible and it cannot be done! If the strongest force of wind cannot get the man to remove a single piece of clothing, then surely the challenge cannot be accomplished!"

14 The North Wind retreated behind the mountain and watched the Sun. He chuckled to himself as the Sun came out from behind the cloud.

15 The Sun rose in the sky. It warmed the air and brightened the road for the traveling man. As the Sun continued to shine brightly, the road became very warm and the man unbuttoned his coat.

16 The Sun grew brighter and brighter. Soon the man felt so hot he took his coat off and sat down in a shady spot along the road.

17 The North Wind was astonished and confused. "How did you do that?"

18 "It was easy," said the Sun. "I lit the day with gentleness. Sometimes you do not need strength to be strong."

19 The North Wind could not believe that the Sun had won the competition. He was upset since he knew that he was no longer the most powerful force in nature.

20 The Clouds, Snow, and Rain, and all of the other weather, congratulated the Sun. They cheered, "You are the most powerful of all weather!"

21 But the Sun, being wise and humble, reminded them that all weather was important in its own special way. "Each of us does an important job, and each of us depends on the other to create the seasons. None of us is more powerful than the rest. We all have an important job to do in our own way."

22 The Sun reached out to the North Wind and explained that we all should feel proud in the work that we do. The North Wind finally understood what the Sun had been trying to say all along.

7. **Part A.** What does the word **boast** mean as it is used in paragraph 5 of "The North Wind and the Sun"?

O A. The North Wind thought he was stronger than anyone else.
O B. The North Wind was angry at the Sun.
O C. The North Wind was worried that he might not be powerful.
O D. The North Wind was afraid that he might lose the competition.

Part B. Which sentence **best** supports the answer to Part A?

O A. "The Sun, however, continued to protest this claim and argued that there was power in gentleness." (paragraph 5)
O B. "He would brag to everyone he met about his great power and strength." (paragraph 5)
O C. "But the North Wind did not understand how something could be both strong and gentle." (paragraph 5)
O D. "The Sun rested behind a cloud and watched the North Wind at work." (paragraph 10)

8. **Part A.** Why did the North Wind start to blow in paragraph 12?

O A. The North Wind wanted to knock down a tree.
O B. The North Wind wanted the man's coat to come off.
O C. The North Wind wanted to blow the leaves on the ground.
O D. The North Wind was annoyed with the Sun.

Part B. Based on your answer to Part A, what was the effect of the North Wind blowing?

O A. The Sun went behind a cloud.
O B. Trees began to fall down.
O C. The man fell down to the ground.
O D. The man held his coat tighter.

9. Complete the chart to identify the moral of "The North Wind and the Sun." Provide a supporting detail for the moral.

Select the **best** moral for "The North Wind and the Sun" from the selections below and write it in the chart:

One good turn deserves another.
One can be gentle and strong at the same time.
Being boastful shows strength.

Select a detail that **best** supports the moral you selected.

"It was easy," said the Sun. "I lit the day with gentleness. Sometimes you do not need strength to be strong."
The Sun announced, "I see a way to end our dispute. We shall have a contest."
"As a test of strength," said the Sun, "let us see which of us can take the coat off that man. You begin."

Moral of the Story:	
Supporting Detail:	

The Three Brothers

A Folktale from Nagaland

1 Long ago, there lived three brothers. They had a small farm and little cottage in which they lived. The eldest brother, Tanyen, worked hard on the farm while his lazy and selfish brothers, Zhoshu and Penhun, ate and slept all day.

2 It was difficult to meet the needs of the family with such a **meager** income. Tanyen said to his brothers, "It's not possible to carry on like this, brothers! I will go out and seek my fortune. I will become rich so I can provide for both of you." Tanyen began to prepare for his journey. He began to pack his work tools and gather his supplies. He mapped out a route for his travels. Zhoshu and Penhun didn't like the idea.

3 "Why should Tanyen become rich?" they said to each other. "We should go out and seek our fortune, too!"

4 So, the selfish brothers devised a plan and went to Tanyen. "Brother, I have realized my responsibilities," said Zhoshu. "I will go out, seek my fortune, and become rich so I can help our family, too."

5 "As you wish, dear Zhoshu!" replied Tanyen. That day at breakfast, Zhoshu pretended to be very loving and caring.

6 "Eat well, Penhun," he said, "and don't worry; I shall soon return rich!"

7 He then took leave of his brothers and started on his journey. He kept walking throughout the day. By late evening, hungry and tired, he reached another village.

8 He went up to a hut and knocked at the door. An old woman answered, "Who's there?"

9 "I'm a traveler," Zhoshu replied. "Can I stay here for the night?"

10 "Only if you remove all the stars from that pool!" said the old woman, pointing to a pool of water.

11 Zhoshu thought, "How can I remove those stars? They are nothing but a reflection of the sky!" Puzzled and exhausted, he returned home and said to his family, "I couldn't find my fortune anywhere!"

12 Next, Penhun decided to try his luck and left home. Wandering, he too reached the old woman's hut and was asked to fish out the stars from the pool. "How is that possible?" he thought and returned home. "Nowhere could I find my fortune," he said sadly.

13 Now it was Tenyan's turn. When he reached the old woman's hut, he too was asked to perform the same task. He humbly asked for a bucket, which the old woman gave him. Tanyen stepped into the pool and began to throw out bucketfuls of water. He worked hard all night, until the pool was completely dry.

14 In the morning when the old woman came out of her hut, Tanyen showed her the dry pit and said, "I have removed all the stars!"

15 The old woman was pleased. She led him to a huge farm and said, "This is your reward. From today, you are the owner of this farm!" Tanyen thanked the old woman and returned home a rich man.

16 "I have found my fortune!" he announced.

17 "But where?" asked his brothers.

18 "I found it in my own hands!" replied Tanyen. He then told them all that had happened. His lazy brothers resolved to work hard from that day. And they lived happily for the rest of their lives.

10. Part A. What is the **best** meaning for the word **meager** as it is used in paragraph 2 of the story, shown below.

> It was difficult to meet the needs of the family with such a **meager** income. Tanyen said to his brothers, "It's not possible to carry on like this, brothers! I will go out and seek my fortune. I will become rich so I can provide for both of you." Tanyen began to prepare for his journey. He began to pack his work tools and gather his supplies. He mapped out a route for his travels. Zhoshu and Penhun didn't like the idea.

O A. Not having enough
O B. Having enough
O C. Having too much
O D. Being satisfied

Part B. Which detail from paragraph 2 **best** supports your answer to Part A?

O A. "He began to pack his work tools and gather his supplies."
O B. "It was difficult to meet the needs of the family"
O C. "He mapped out a route for his travels."
O D. "Zhoshu and Penhun didn't like the idea."

11. Part A. What is the moral of "The Three Brothers"?

O A. Sometimes you have to ask others to help you.
O B. You should be happy with what you have.
O C. Hard work gets rewarded.
O D. You can't have everything you want

Part B. Which detail from the story **best** supports your answer to Part A?

O A. "Zhoshu thought, 'How can I remove those stars? They are nothing but a reflection of the sky!'" (paragraph 11)
O B. "'How is that possible?' he thought and returned home. 'Nowhere could I find my fortune!' he said sadly." (paragraph 12)
O C. "The old woman was pleased. She led him to a huge farm and said, 'This is your reward. From today, you are the owner of this farm!'" (paragraph 15)
O D. "'Eat well, Penhun,' he said, 'and don't worry; I shall soon return rich!'" (paragraph 6)

12. Part A. Which statement **best** describes what the picture adds to the story?

- O A. The picture shows that the brothers are tired from working so hard.
- O B. The picture shows that Tanyen is working hard while his brothers are being lazy.
- O C. The picture shows Tanyen looking for something.
- O D. The picture shows how the brothers took the stars from the pool of water.

Part B. Which sentence from the story **best** supports the answer to Part A?

- O A. "His lazy brothers resolved to work hard from that day. And they lived happily for the rest of their lives." (paragraph 18)
- O B. "The eldest brother, Tanyen, worked hard on the farm while his lazy and selfish brothers, Zhoshu and Penhun, ate and slept all day." (paragraph 1)
- O C. "In the morning when the old woman came out of her hut, Tanyen showed her the dry pit and said, 'I have removed all the stars.'" (paragraph 14)
- O D. "Puzzled and exhausted, he returned home and said to his family, 'I couldn't find my fortune anywhere!'" (paragraph 11)

13. "The Wind and the Sun" and "The Three Brothers" both try to teach important lessons to the characters in the stories. Write an essay that explains how "The North Wind and the Sun" and "The Three Brothers" each teach a lesson. Write about the moral or lesson from each story. Compare and contrast both folktales by using what you learned about the characters. Include descriptions, words, actions, and specific details from both stories, to support your ideas.

Research Simulation Task

Article 1

Directions: There are important ways that people can help the environment. Today you will research some ways you can help our environment. You will read two articles that will help you with your research.

As you read these texts, you will gather information and answer questions about the ways to help our environment. Then you will be asked to write an essay about what you have learned.

Read the article "Kids to the Rescue" and answer the questions that follow.

Kids to the Rescue

1 Taking care of our environment is an important job, and it's not just a job for grown-ups. There is something for everyone, including children, to do.

2 Some things you can do on your own, some with a friend, and others with the help of an adult. Just look around your neighborhood or school, and think about ways to improve the environment. It is never too late to begin. Here are a few ideas to help you get started.

3 Keep your neighborhood clean and beautiful. If your parents own a car, make litter bags for them. Keep your yard free of trash. You can also help organize clean-up days in your community and school.

4 You can help out in your school, too. If your school playground doesn't have a garbage can, ask the principal or custodian to put one out. You can also start a recycling program in the cafeteria. Make posters reminding other students to put garbage where it belongs. Create a bulletin board showing pictures of clean areas and other areas spoiled by litter or trash.

5 Kids can make a difference by "reducing," "reusing," and "recycling," often referred to as the 3 R's. They need to educate themselves and others about ways to promote the 3 R's. Environmental clubs encourage groups of children to work together to protect our planet. Some clubs sponsor school-wide environmental education programs and events.

6 There are many benefits when you become earth-friendly and make a point to use the 3 R's each day. The three R's all help to cut down on the amount of waste we throw away. When we throw less waste away we **conserve** natural resources, landfill space, and energy. When we conserve something we take care of it and use it wisely.

7 When you reduce, reuse, and recycle you save money, less goes to waste and more is left for others, you make the environment a cleaner and better place to live. Most important, using the 3 R's is the right thing to do!

Adapted from *New York State Grade 4 Elementary-Level English Language Arts Test*, by Debora S. Whiting and Donna C. Oliverio (Barron's, 2007)

14. **Part A.** What does the word **conserve** mean as it is used in paragraph 6?

O A. protect
O B. destroy
O C. plant
O D. waste

Part B. According to paragraph 6, what is one way we can conserve?

O A. Use a lot of products.
O B. Throw old clothes away.
O C. Throw less waste away.
O D. Take things to the landfill.

15. **Part A.** What is the main idea of this article?

O A. Kids can help the environment.
O B. Keeping the environment clean is hard work.
O C. You should join a club at school.
O D. Your parents should visit the landfill.

Part B. What detail from the article **best** supports your answer to Part A?

O A. "The three R's all help to cut down on the amount of waste we throw away." (paragraph 6)
O B. "When you reduce, reuse, and recycle you save money, less goes to waste and more is left for others, you make the environment a cleaner and better place to live. (paragraph 7)
O C. "Taking care of our environment is an important job, and it's not just a job for grown-ups." (paragraph 1)
O D. "When we conserve something we take care of it and use it wisely." (paragraph 6)

16. Complete the graphic organizer below using key details from the article "Kids to the Rescue."

Key Details

Organize a clean-up day in your town.

Start a recycling program in the cafeteria.

Make litter bags for automobiles.

Ask the custodian to place a garbage can out in the playground.

How Kids Can Make a Difference in the Community Environment	How Kids Can Make a Difference in the School Environment

Article 2

Directions: Read the article "Reduce, Reuse, Recycle" and answer the questions that follow.

Reduce, Reuse, Recycle

1 Reduce, Reuse, Recycle—Three great ways YOU can eliminate waste and protect your environment!

2 Waste, and how we choose to handle it, affects our world's environment—that's YOUR **environment**. The environment is everything around you, including the air, water, land, plants, and man-made things. And since by now you probably know that you need a healthy environment for your own health and happiness, you can understand why effective waste management is so important to YOU and everyone else. The waste we create has to be carefully controlled to be sure that it does not harm your environment and your health.

What exactly is "waste?"

3 Waste is anything we throw away or get rid of, that doesn't get used.

How can you help?

4 You can help by learning about and practicing the three R's of waste management: **Reduce, reuse, and recycle!** Practicing all three of these activities every day is not only important for a healthy environment, but it can also be fun. So let's take a minute right now to learn more about waste and waste management, so you can become a key player in making our world a safe and healthy place.

- **Reduce.** Reduce or limit the amount of new stuff you buy. To reduce waste, buy things that have less packaging. Use a dishcloth instead of paper towels. Use both sides of a piece of paper when you write.
- **Reuse.** Try to borrow or rent things you'll only need for a short amount of time, and reuse the things you already have. When you have things you no longer need, give them to others who can use them. Use reusable bags when you go shopping. Donate old clothes. Use glassware instead of paper products.
- **Recycle.** Remember to recycle whatever materials you can, like bottles, cans, and paper, so they can be collected and remade into new products.
- **Buy recycled.** Choose products made from recycled materials whenever you can.

The rewards of recycling

5 Recycling and reusing has many benefits. It helps to save energy, conserves natural resources, and limits pollution. Recycling and reusing items also save you money!

Facts about our environment

6 If you still are not convinced that recycling and reusing products are important, check out these facts!

- ✔ Every year nearly 900,000,000 trees are cut down to provide materials for American paper and products. That's 900 BILLION!
- ✔ Americans throw away about 28 billion bottles and jars every year.
- ✔ Americans make more than 200 million tons of garbage each year!
- ✔ It takes a 15-year-old tree to produce 700 grocery bags.
- ✔ Disposable diapers last centuries in landfills. An average baby will go through 8,000 of them!

7 Each year Americans throw away 25,000,000,000 Styrofoam cups. Even 500 years from now, the foam coffee cup you used this morning will be sitting in a landfill.

8 Recycling is an important part to saving our environment and saving our resources. Our world depends on it. It is never too late to get started!

Source: *http://kids.niehs.nih.gov/explore/reduce/*

17. Part A. What does the word **environment** mean as it is used in paragraph 2?

O A. recycling materials
O B. everything around you
O C. conserving water
O D. using the landfills

Part B. What detail from the article **best** supports your answer to Part A?

O A. ". . . you need a healthy environment . . ." (paragraph 2)
O B. ". . . including the air, water, land, plants, and man-made things." (paragraph 2)
O C. ". . . waste we create has to be carefully controlled . . ." (paragraph 2)
O D. ". . . so you can become a key player in making our world a safe and healthy place." (paragraph 4)

18. Part A. According to this article, what are **two** benefits from recycling?

☐ A. It helps to save energy.
☐ B. It is the law.
☐ C. It can be fun to do with a friend.
☐ D. It can cause pollution.
☐ E. If we do not recycle we will have to use plastic bags.
☐ F. It can save us money.

Part B. Which **bolded** heading in the article helped you answer Part A?

O A. **What exactly is "waste?"**
O B. **How can you help?**
O C. **The rewards of recycling**
O D. **Facts about our environment**

19. According to this article, what are some ways you can reduce, reuse, and recycle? Select three examples of ways to reduce, reuse, and recycle from the list of possible answers. Write the letter to the answers you selected in the box below.

Possible answers:

A. Use a dishcloth instead of paper towels.

B. Use paper plates and cups.

C. Donate old clothes.

D. Reuse bags from stores.

E. Throw all trash in the garbage.

Ways to Reduce, Reuse, and Recycle		

20. You have just read two texts about ways to help the environment. Both "Kids to the Rescue" and "Reduce, Reuse, Recycle" provide information on ways kids can help. Think about the information each article provides on the topic. Write an essay explaining how kids can help the environment. Be sure to include things kids can do at home and at school. Remember to use text evidence from both articles to support your ideas. Your response should

- introduce the topic and logically organize the information;
- include appropriate supporting details from both passages;
- use words and phrases to link different ideas;
- use correct spelling, grammar, and punctuation.

Answers

Narrative Writing Task

"The Mermaids"

1. **Part A. C** *Two mermaids were playing in the water.* The splashing that Maggie heard in paragraph 2 of the story were the mermaids.

   Part B. A *Then, suddenly, two heads came into view.* This detail best supports the answer for Part A that the splashing was coming from the mermaids.

2. **Part A. D** One day, something in the waves caught her eye means *She noticed something in the ocean.* Sometimes you will need to continue reading to help you figure out the meaning. Paragraph 2 describes all the things that "caught her eye."

   Part B. C *She heard laughter, splashing, and talking coming from the ocean.* This answer supports the answer for Part A that there were mermaids in the water.

3. **Part A. B** *Maggie had never seen a mermaid before.* When Maggie saw the mermaids, she was **most likely** surprised because she had never seen a mermaid before. This is stated directly in paragraph 6.

   Part B. A *Was she really talking to mermaids?* (paragraph 6) If you reread paragraph 6 you will discover that she has never seen a mermaid before. She could not believe she was talking to a real mermaid. If paragraph numbers are listed, go back and reread the entire section to be sure your answer supports Part A.

4. **Part A. C** Olivia and Loretta stayed away from Maggie when she brought her sister because Maggie's sister had a camera to take a picture of the mermaids.

   Part B. D and F **D:** *"The king of our land has warned us never to let humans see that we exist."*

   F: *But, if the story was true, she was going to take a picture to show everyone that mermaids really do exist.*

   Both of these sentences are reasons the mermaids stayed away when Maggie's sister arrived.

5.

What Happens in the Story?

In the beginning, Maggie meets two mermaids at the beach.
Next, Maggie tells her sister about the mermaids.
Then, the mermaids do not show up when Maggie's sister comes to see them.
At the end, Maggie promises not to tell anyone that the mermaids are real.

6. Refer to the Narrative Writing Scoring Rubric in the Appendix. Sample response:

Journal Entry

2-10-15

Today was certainly an interesting day! It was a beautiful day and the sun was shining brightly. I ran toward the ocean and sat on the wooden bench waiting for my friends to pop up from the salty ocean. Over the last few weeks we have become such good friends. They even taught me a few new tricks in the water! As I was sitting on the bench, I saw two heads pop up! I was so excited! There they were—Olivia with her long red hair and blue sparkling eyes and Loretta with dark hair and green eyes that were the color of the water. They both smiled and waved at me. I quickly threw my towel on the bench and dove off the pier.

Then, while in the water, we saw dolphins come up to us. They wanted to play, too! Olivia and Loretta seemed to be able to communicate with them. Suddenly, we were all playing and splashing in the water. I heard the roaring sound coming from under the waves and I knew it was time for them to go to school. As I said goodbye to them, both of my friends waved their fins and dove into the deep waters. All of a sudden I heard a sound coming from the bushes by the bench. It was my sister Maggie! She had a surprised look on her face. She had finally seen the mermaids and knew they were real!

I asked her to keep the secret from mom and dad and she agreed to. I also asked her not to take pictures and explained how the king of the mermaids was afraid to let humans know they existed. To my surprise, Maggie totally understood. Maybe someday I will be able to introduce my sister to the mermaids. I sure hope so! But for now, it will be our secret!

Literary Task

"The North Wind and the Sun"

7. Part A. A *The North Wind thought he was stronger than anyone else.* In the story the North Wind thinks he is the most powerful. Remember that when a paragraph number is mentioned in the question, you must go back and reread the paragraph. If you still are not sure of the answer, read the paragraphs that come before and after.

Part B. B *He would brag to everyone he met about his great power and strength.* This answer supports Part A, that the North Wind thought he was stronger than anyone else.

8. Part A. B *The Wind started to blow because he wanted to take the man's coat off.* The Sun and the North Wind were in a competition. The North Wind was blowing to try to get the man to take off his coat.

Part B. D *The man held his coat tighter.* Part A mentions paragraph 12 in the question. Be sure to read the paragraph. At the end of the paragraph it stated that the man clenched his coat tighter. The reason he was holding his coat tighter was because the wind was blowing so strongly.

9. Moral of the Story: *One can be gentle and strong at the same time.*

Supporting Detail: *"It was easy," said the Sun. "I lit the day with gentleness. Sometimes you do not need strength to be strong."*

Keep in mind that this question is asking you to select the best answer. Think about the problem and how it was solved when considering a moral. The North Wind could not understand how something could be both strong and gentle at the same time.

"The Three Brothers"

10. Part A. A *Not having enough* In the story, Tanyen was worried that their income was not enough. He went out to seek his fortune to help his family.

Part B. B *It was difficult to meet the needs of the family.* This answer best supports Part A. It was difficult to meet the needs of the family because they had a "meager" income, or not enough income.

11. Part A. C *Hard work gets rewarded.* Zhoshu and Penhun did not want to think of a way to remove the stars from the pool. They were too lazy and gave up quickly. Tanyen worked all night taking water out of the pool. He knew that if he emptied the pool the stars would be gone. His reward was a huge farm and he became a rich man.

Part B. C *The old woman was pleased. She led him to a huge farm and said, "This is your reward. From today, you are the owner of this farm!"* This answer supports the moral that hard work gets rewarded.

12. Part A. B *The picture shows that Tanyen is working hard while his brothers are being lazy.* The story does not state that the brothers worked hard or that Tanyen was looking for something as stated in choices A and C. Additionally, the brothers were not able to take the stars from the pool of water as stated in choice D. The correct answer is B, since the evidence in the text supports this selection.

Part B. B *The eldest brother, Tanyen, worked hard on the farm while his lazy and selfish brothers, Zhoshu and Penhun, ate and slept all day.* This selection accurately describes the scene in the illustration. Both brothers are asleep under the tree while Tanyen is working hard.

13. Refer to the Literary Analysis Scoring Rubric in the Appendix. Sample Response:

Stories from across the world can help teach a lesson. We can learn a lot from the characters and how they interact. We can also learn from the problems they face and especially from how their problems are resolved. "The North Wind and the Sun" and "The Three Brothers" are both folktales that teach valuable lessons.

The first story, "The North Wind and the Sun," described how the North Wind would brag about his strength. He really thought he was stronger than anyone else. The Sun, however, tried to convince him that there was power in being gentle. The North Wind just could not understand how something could be gentle and powerful at the same time. They both agreed to have a contest. The Sun said, "As a test of strength, let us see which of us can take off the coat of the man." The man was walking down the road and felt the North Wind blow, but he only closed his coat tighter. The North Wind gave up. Now it was the Sun's turn. The Sun turned up the heat. It became so hot that the man took off his coat! At the end of the story, the Sun said, "Sometimes you do not need strength to be strong." The moral of this story is that strength can come from being gentle.

The second text, "The Three Brothers," also teaches a lesson. Unlike "The North Wind and the Sun," this folktale teaches the importance of hard work. In the story, Tanyen's brothers are lazy and give up quickly. Unlike his brothers, Tanyen worked very hard. When he was asked to remove the stars from the old woman's pool, he worked all night to do so. In the story it says "He worked hard all night, until the pool was completely dry." His reward was a huge farm. The moral of this story is that hard work will be rewarded.

In the end, each story taught us a different lesson. The Sun taught the North Wind that there was power in being gentle. And in the second story, Tanyen taught his brothers that you need to work hard to get what you want. Finally, both stories are similar because the characters in both stories go through a challenge to prove themselves.

"Kids to the Rescue"

14. Part A. A *protect* The word **conserve** means to protect something. We want to conserve or protect our environment.

Part B. C *throw less waste away* Paragraph 6 states that when we throw less waste away we conserve natural resources. Always make certain that when a paragraph number is mentioned, you reread the *entire* paragraph before answering.

15. Part A. A *Kids can help the environment.* The article discusses many ways that kids can help the environment.

Part B. C *Taking care of our environment is an important job, and it's not just a job for grown-ups.* This sentence supports the main idea in Part A that kids can help the environment.

16. Part A.

How Kids Can Make a Difference in the Community Environment	How Kids Can Make a Difference in the School Environment
Organize a clean-up day in your town.	Start a recycling program in the cafeteria.
Make litter bags for automobiles.	Ask the custodian to place a garbage can out in the playground.

These are all details that can be found in paragraphs 3 and 4 of the article.

"Reduce, Reuse, Recycle"

17. Part A. B *Everything around you* The word **environment** means everything around you. Reread paragraph 2. Remember, when a paragraph number is mentioned in the question, you should go back and reread the entire paragraph.

Part B. B *The environment is everything around you, including the air, water, land, plants, and man-made things.* This statement best supports the idea in Part A that the environment is everything that is around you. Be sure to use what the text says when answering. Do not be fooled by selecting an answer because *you* know what the word means; you need to think about how it is used in the text, and then go back and reread the section to make sure you are selecting the **best** answer.

18. Part A. A and F *It helps to save energy. It can save us money.* Paragraph 5 states that recycling has many benefits, such as saving energy and saving money. The other answers are not supported by text evidence.

Part B. C *The rewards of recycling* This bolded heading in the text is the only answer choice that would provide details about the benefits of recycling. The other choices focus on waste, ways to help, and facts.

19.

Ways to Reduce, Reuse, and Recycle		
A. Use a dishcloth instead of paper towels.	C. Donate old clothes.	D. Reuse bags from stores.

Using paper plates and cups is not a way to reduce, reuse, or recycle. Throwing all trash in the garage is a good idea, but it is not a way to reduce, reuse, or recycle. Always focus on what the question is asking you and what the text says. Do not be tricked by answers you think are good, but that do not answer the question.

20. Refer to the Research Simulation Task Scoring Rubric in the Appendix. Sample Response:

Have you ever thought about what would happen to our environment if no one took care of it? If we do not do our part in helping, the environment could run out of natural resources and our landfills could become too full. The good news is that kids can do a lot to help save the environment!

The article "Kids to the Rescue" mentions things you can do in your neighborhood and at your school. You can keep your neighborhood clean by picking up trash and, according to this article, you can also help organize clean-up days in your community. If you wanted to help out with the environment in school, you could start a recycling program in the cafeteria or make posters reminding other students to pick up garbage.

The article "Reduce, Reuse, Recycle" also gives some ideas on ways to protect the environment by getting rid of waste. This article says that Americans throw away about 28 billion bottles and jars every year. The article tells us how reducing, reusing, and recycling can help. The author gives some ways kids can help too. "To reduce waste, buy things that have less packaging. Use a dishcloth instead of paper towels. Use both sides of a piece of paper when you write." Also, you can reuse things instead of throwing them out. For example, you can donate old clothes. Finally, you can recycle bottles and cans so they can be made into new products. Kids have the power to make a difference!

Practice Test for EBSR and TECR Questions

Now you will take a practice test to help you prepare for EBSR and TECR questions. EBSR and TECR questions are provided to you in this section for additional practice and to help strengthen your skills on answering these types of questions on the PARCC.

To answer the questions on this practice test, you will first be asked to read two texts. Read each text and the questions that follow very carefully. Then choose the best answer for each question. You may look back at the passages as often as necessary.

Identify your answers by selecting from the answer choices. If you do not know the answer to the question, skip it and go on. If time permits, you may return to questions in this practice test. Do your best to answer every question.

PRACTICE TEST FOR EBSR AND TECR QUESTIONS

Directions: Read the story "The Golfing Champions." Pay close attention to the actions of the characters and the events in the story. Answer questions 1 through 5. You may look back at the passage as often as necessary.

The Golfing Champions

By Emma Baker

1 My name is David and I am a middle child in my family. I also have two little sisters, Danielle and Sarah. They are twins. I have one big sister, too. Her name is Amy. She is old enough to drive, which can sometimes come in handy. My family really enjoys spending time together. All of my sisters have activities they enjoy doing, such as cheerleading, softball, and soccer, but my father and I love to play golf. I would have to say that golf is my passion! I practice a lot in order to improve my golf swing. I usually practice at the miniature golf course a few miles from my house. My father and I play at championship tournaments and sometimes we even win!

2 You need to practice a lot to win a championship. But sometimes practicing is hard. Well, actually it's not the practicing that's hard. The hard part can be getting to the golf course! Some days that is harder than others! This is the story of one really hard practice!

3 "Mom," I said, as I was quickly eating my breakfast, "I'm going to the miniature golf course to meet Dad."

4 "Okay," said Mom. "Take Danielle and Sara with you."

5 "Do I have…." I stopped. I knew the answer.

6 "I am busy, though. Who is driving you?" asked Mom.

7 "Amy," I said as I finished putting on my sneakers. I knew this wasn't going to go smoothly. My sister Amy is always busy with her friends and doesn't exactly like driving us younger kids to our practices.

8 "WHAT?" said Amy, stomping out of her room. "I am not driving a bunch of little kids to the golf course. I am going to meet my friends at the China Town Restaurant to have lunch."

9 "But, Mom," I said. "I have to go to the golf course. Dad signed us up for the championship and this will be our last day for training before the championship. I have to go!"

10 "A-a-m-m-y-y," Mom said in a voice that told Amy she had no choice.

11 "Fine," yelled Amy. "I'll drive you. Let's go."

12 Now, maybe you are thinking my troubles ended there. Wrong. The championship match was the next day. Dad wanted the family to drive to the golf course together in the family van. I waited patiently looking at the clock and finally it was time to go. Everyone was ready to go; everyone, that is, except Amy.

13 "Come on, let's go!" Dad and I yelled. "We need to go now."

14 "Wait, where is Amy?" Mom asked. We went through the house frantically searching for her.

15 Just then, we all heard the water running in the shower. Amy was not even dressed yet!

16 "M-m-o-m-m," I said. "Make her hurry. We will be late. We can't be late. We can't win if we are late. Make her hurry. Please."

17 Mom went upstairs and talked to Amy. Five minutes later, we were all in the van. We came to a sign that said Golden Golf Course. My heart began to race.

18 "Wow, this is amazing," I said. "It's so cool!" The place was enormous and there was a long line at the registration table. The organizers of the event placed us in teams.

19 The teams were standing together, and it was time to start the game.

20 Six hours later, Dad and I were tied for first place. It was 72 to 72. Dad and I could win the match if we won this hole.

21 My dad shot first. He did great. Now it was up to me! I gripped my golf club. I got scared that we were going to lose. The final shot all depended on me! I looked over at the huge trophy. I heard my dad say, "You can make this shot."

22 Everyone yelled and cheered. I made it. Dad and I won the championship. Dad and I stood there with the trophy as my family gathered around. Mom, Danielle, Sarah, and . . . Amy. She said she wouldn't have missed this for the world!

From *New York State Grade 3 Elementary-Level English Language Arts Test*, by Jane A. Gallant (Barron's, 2008)

1. **Part A.** According to David, who caused most of the problems in this story?

O A. the twins, Danielle and Sarah
O B. David's sister, Amy
O C. David
O D. Dad

Part B. Which **two** details from the passage **best** support the answer to Part A?

☐ A. "I am not driving a bunch of little kids to the golf course." (paragraph 8)
☐ B. "Dad signed us up for the championship . . ." (paragraph 9)
☐ C. "Just then, we all heard the water running in the shower." (paragraph 15)
☐ D. ". . . and it was time to start the game." (paragraph 19)
☐ E. "I heard my dad say, 'You can make this shot.'" (paragraph 21)
☐ F. "Take Danielle and Sara with you." (paragraph 4)

2. **Part A.** Read the following sentence from the story:

"WHAT?" said Amy stomping out of her room.

This sentence **most likely** means that:

O A. Amy was happy to drive the children to the golf course.
O B. Amy did not hear what David said.
O C. Amy did not want to drive the children to the golf course.
O D. Amy was surprised to hear what David said.

Part B. Which detail from the passage **best** supports the answer to Part A?

O A. "Wow, this is amazing." (paragraph 18)
O B. "Take Danielle and Sara with you." (paragraph 4)
O C. "I am going to meet my friends at the China Town Restaurant to have lunch." (paragraph 8)
O D. "Wait, where is Amy?" (paragraph 14)

3. **Part A.** According to the information in this story, why was David upset when his sister was in the shower?

O A. It was his turn to use the shower.
O B. Amy was using all the hot water.
O C. Amy is late for everything.
O D. He was worried he would miss the championship.

Part B. Which detail from the passage **best** supports the answer to Part A?

O A. "We can't win if we are late." (paragraph 16)
O B. "Five minutes later, we were all in the van." (paragraph 17)
O C. "... this will be our last day for training before the championship." (paragraph 9)
O D. "I'm going to the miniature golf course to meet Dad." (paragraph 3)

4. **Part A.** How did David feel about participating in the golfing championship toward the end of the story?

O A. David was nervous.
O B. David was sure he would win.
O C. David was tired from practicing.
O D. David did not want to compete in the championship.

Part B. What detail from the story **best** supports your answer to Part A?

O A. "I got scared that we were going to lose." (paragraph 21)
O B. "Wow, this is amazing." (paragraph 18)
O C. "Come on, let's go!" (paragraph 13)
O D. "The hard part can be getting to the golf course!" (paragraph 2)

5. Place the following key details in the order in which they occur in the story you just read:

David and his father win the golf championship.

David goes to the miniature golf course to practice with his dad.

The family drives to the Golden Golf Course.

Amy is in the shower when everyone is ready to leave.

What Happens in the Story?

Directions: Read the following text called "A Tail Comes in Handy." Answer the questions that follow. You may look back at the passage as often as necessary.

A Tail Comes in Handy

1 Animals use their tails for different purposes. You can learn fascinating information about animals just from observing their tails.

How Are Tails Used for Communication?

2 Animals such as wolves and ostrich use their tails to show rank among the group. A timid wolf will keep its tail between its legs, whereas a fearless wolf will raise its tail. The highest-ranking male ostrich will hold his tail pointing straight up to show his dominance. The next-highest-ranking male will hold his tail horizontal, while other birds droop their tails down to show they are **subordinate**, or less important than other birds.

3 Deer also use their tails to communicate with each other. A white-tailed deer will lift its tail straight up and wag it, showing the white fur underneath. The white fur acts like an alarm or signal, which warns other deer of approaching danger.

How Are Tails Used for Balance?

4 The kangaroo and the squirrel use their tails for balance. A kangaroo's tail acts like a third leg; it allows the animal to prop itself up. The squirrel's bushy tail not only provides warmth on winter days, but it also helps the animal keep its balance when it is leaping and climbing.

How Are Tails Used for Movement?

5 Birds use their tails to move around and balance on branches. Most fish have tails that help them with movement and direction.

How Are Tails Used to Scare Off Predators?

6 Many animals use their tails to give a warning that they feel threatened and are ready to defend themselves. To warn would-be attackers, a rattlesnake will rattle its tail and a porcupine will raise its quills and shake them. A ground iguana scares off its enemies by whipping its tail fiercely. Horses, giraffes, cows, and lions have tails that can swat off the peskiest of flies. Tails serve many purposes for all kinds of animals.

From *New York State Grade 4 Elementary-Level English Language Arts Test*, by Debora S. Whiting and Donna C. Oliverio (Barron's, 2007)

6. **Part A.** What does the word **subordinate** mean, as it is used in paragraph 2?

O A. higher ranking
O B. lower ranking
O C. mean
O D. very strong

Part B. What detail from the text **best** supports your answer choice to Part A?

O A. ". . . help them with movement and direction." (paragraph 5)
O B. ". . . less important than other birds." (paragraph 2)
O C. ". . . to move around and balance on branches." (paragraph 5)
O D. ". . . warns other deer of approaching danger." (paragraph 3)

7. **Part A.** According to this article, how do tails come in handy for movement?

O A. Birds use their tails to get around.
O B. Wolves use their tails to go through the woods.
O C. Kangaroos use their tails like a third leg.
O D. Ostrich point their tails straight up.

Part B. Which detail **best** supports your answer to Part A?

O A. ". . . to show rank among the group." (paragraph 2)
O B. ". . . to move around and balance on branches." (paragraph 5)
O C. ". . . it allows the animal to prop itself up." (paragraph 4)
O D. ". . . will lift its tail straight up and wag it . . ." (paragraph 3)

8. **Part A.** The article suggests that animals use their tails to scare off predators. Which animal uses its tail to scare off predators?

O A. ostrich
O B. wolf
O C. porcupine
O D. squirrel

Part B. What sentence from the text **best** supports your answer to Part A?

O A. ". . . when it is leaping and climbing." (paragraph 4)
O B. ". . . to show rank among the group." (paragraph 2)
O C. ". . . while other birds droop their tails. . . ." (paragraph 2)
O D. ". . . will raise its quills and shake them." (paragraph 6)

9. **Part A.** According to this article, how does a ground iguana keep enemies away?

O A. by raising its quills and shaking them
O B. by making a hissing sound
O C. by whipping its tail fiercely
O D. by pointing its tail straight up

Part B. Which section of the passage provides information about the answer to Part A?

O A. How Are Tails Used for Movement?
O B. How Are Tails Used for Communication?
O C. How Are Tails Used for Balance?
O D. How Are Tails Used to Scare Off Predators?

10. Part A. According to this article, how do deer use their tails?

O A. for movement
O B. to show rank
O C. for balancing
O D. to communicate

Part B. Which detail from the text **best** supports your answer to Part A?

O A. ". . . which warns other deer of approaching danger." (paragraph 3)
O B. ". . . it allows the animal to prop itself up." (paragraph 4)
O C. ". . . helps the animal keep its balance . . ." (paragraph 4)
O D. ". . . use their tails to move around and balance on branches." (paragraph 5)

11. Select the main idea of the article you just read and write it in the box labeled Main Idea. Then choose **two** details that best support the main idea. Write the answers in the boxes labeled Supporting Detail 1 and Supporting Detail 2.

Possible Main Ideas	Possible Supporting Details
Tails can help protect against predators.	Tails are used for communication.
Animals use their tails in many ways.	Tails can get stuck in bushes.
Some animals could not survive without tails.	Tails are used for balancing.
	Some tails are long and others are short.

Main Idea:
Supporting Detail 1:
Supporting Detail 2:

12. Using information from the article you just read, select a word to identify how each animal below uses its tail. Write your answer in the chart below. The first one is done for you.

A. warmth
B. signal
C. communicate
D. balance
E. movement

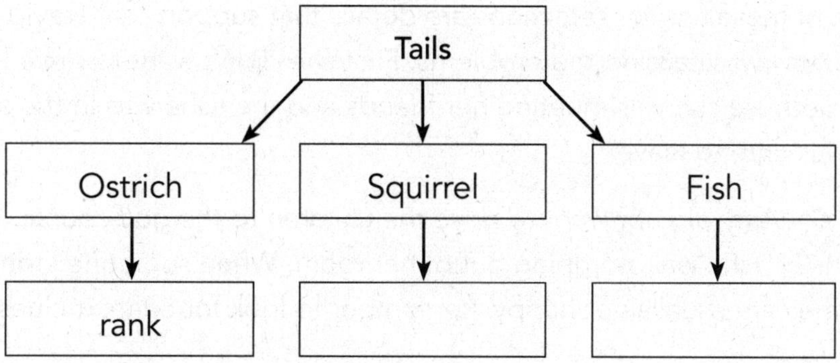

Answers

"The Golfing Champions"

1. **Part A. B** *David's sister Amy* Throughout this story Amy is causing problems for David. First by stating she wasn't driving David to the miniature golf course, and then again by not being ready to leave for the championship on time.

   Part B. A and C *"I am not driving a bunch of little kids to the golf course." (paragraph 8); Just then, we all heard water running in the shower. (paragraph 15)* Both of these answer selections are details that support that David thought his sister Amy was causing the problems. First she didn't want to drive him to practice because she was meeting her friends and then she was in the shower when it was time to leave.

2. **Part A. C** *Amy did not want to drive the children to the golf course.* When Amy said "WHAT?" she was stomping out of her room. When someone stomps out of a room, they are usually not happy. Remember to look for context clues as you read.

   Part B. C *"I am going to meet my friends at the China Town Restaurant to have lunch." (paragraph 8)* This statement supports Part A that Amy did not want to drive the children to the golf course. Be sure to reread the paragraph before you answer to look for evidence to support your choice.

3. **Part A. D** *He was worried he would miss the championship.* This question is asking why he was upset when she was in the shower. The text tells us that they were all ready to leave for the championship.

   Part B. A *We can't win if we are late. (paragraph 16)* This answer is the best detail to support the answer for Part A, that David was afraid he would miss the championship. "We can't win if we are late" is a reason he was worried.

4. **Part A. A** *David was nervous.* Remember the question is asking how David felt towards the end of the story. At the end of the story they were tied for first place. He was nervous.

   Part B. A *I got scared that we were going to lose. (paragraph 21)* This detail supports that he was nervous. The game was tied and it was up to David to make the winning shot.

5.

What Happens in the Story?

David goes to the miniature golf course to practice with his dad.
Amy is in the shower when everyone is ready to leave.
The family drives to the Golden Golf Course.
David and his father win the golf championship.

"A Tail Comes in Handy"

6. **Part A. B** *lower ranking* In paragraph 2, the sentences before the word "subordinate" tell about higher-ranking birds, and then the next-highest-ranking birds. Subordinate comes last because it is the lower ranking.

   Part B. B *. . . less important than other birds.* This sentence supports that the subordinate is a lower-ranking bird. A lower ranking would be less important.

7. **Part A. A** *Birds use their tails to get around.* The article tells how birds use their tails to move and balance on branches. Reread the section on movement before answering the question.

   Part B. B *. . . to move around and balance on branches. (paragraph 5)* The article tells how birds use their tails to move and balance on branches. Reread the section on movement before answering the question.

8. **Part A. C** *porcupine* Although many animals use their tails to scare off animals, porcupines are mentioned in this article.

   Part B. D *. . . will raise its quills and shake them.* This answer shows how a porcupine scares off animals. According to this article, choices A, B, and C are not mentioned as ways to scare off predators.

9. **Part A. C** *by whipping its tail fiercely* The article states that a ground iguana will use its tail to scare off enemies by whipping and shaking it.

   Part B. A *How Are Tails Used to Scare Off Predators?* This heading would be used to find information on how a ground iguana keeps enemies away, since predators are enemies.

10. **Part A. D** *to communicate* The article mentions communication in paragraph 3.

    Part B. A *. . . which warns other deer of approaching danger.* Paragraph 3 states that the white-tailed deer will lift its tail straight up and wag it, showing the white fur underneath. The white fur acts like an alarm or signal, which warns other deer of approaching danger.

11.

Main Idea: Animals use their tails in many ways.
Supporting Detail 1: Tails are used for communication.
Supporting Detail 2: Tails comes in handy for balancing.

12.

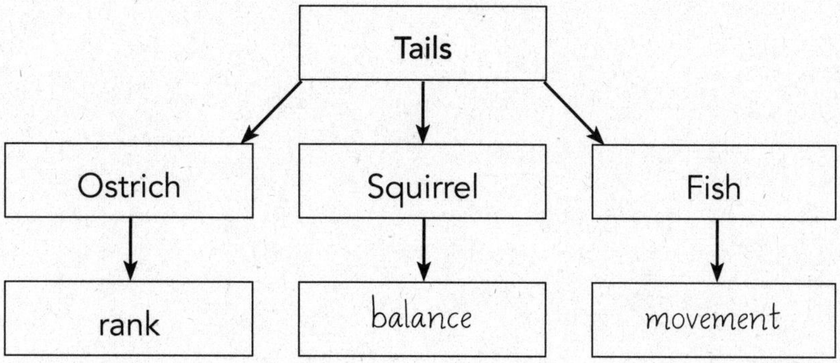

Grade 3 Condensed Scoring Rubric For Prose Constructed-Response Items

APPENDIX A

Narrative Task (NT)

Construct Measured	
Writing Written Expression	
Score Point 3	The student response: • is **effectively** developed with narrative elements and is **consistently appropriate** to the task; • **consistently** demonstrates **purposeful and controlled** organization; • uses language to express ideas with clarity.
Score Point 2	The student response: • is developed with **some** narrative elements and is **generally appropriate** to the task; • demonstrates **purposeful and controlled** organization; • uses language to express ideas with **some** clarity.
Score Point 1	The student response: • is **minimally** developed with **few** narrative elements and is **limited in its appropriateness** to the task; • demonstrates **purposeful** organization that **sometimes is not controlled**; • uses language to express ideas with **limited** clarity.
Score Point 0	The student response: • is **undeveloped** and/or **inappropriate** to the task; • demonstrates **little or no** organization; • does not use language to express ideas with clarity.

Construct Measured	
Writing **Knowledge of Language and Conventions**	
Score Point 3	The student response to the prompt demonstrates **full command** of the conventions of standard English at an appropriate level of complexity. There may be a **few minor errors** in mechanics, grammar, and usage, but **meaning is clear**.
Score Point 2	The student response to the prompt demonstrates **some command** of the conventions of standard English at an appropriate level of complexity. There **may** be errors in mechanics, grammar, and usage that **occasionally impede understanding**, but the **meaning is generally clear**.
Score Point 1	The student response to the prompt demonstrates **limited command** of the conventions of standard English at an appropriate level of complexity. There **may** be errors in mechanics, grammar, and usage that **often impede understanding**.
Score Point 0	The student response to the prompt demonstrates **no command** of the conventions of standard English. **Frequent and varied errors** in mechanics, grammar, and usage **impede understanding**.

NOTE:

- The reading dimension is not scored for elicited narrative stories.
- Per the CCSS, narrative elements in grades 3–5 may include: establishing a situation, organizing a logical event sequence, describing scenes, objects, or people, developing characters' personalities, and using dialogue as appropriate.
- The elements of organization to be assessed are expressed in the grade-level standards W1–W3 and elucidated in the scoring rules for each individual PCR.

Research Simulation Task (RST) and Literary Analysis Task (LAT)

Construct Measured	
Reading **Comprehension of Key Ideas and Details**	
Score Point 3	The student response demonstrates **full comprehension** by providing an **accurate** explanation/description/comparison and by referencing the text(s) explicitly.
Score Point 2	The student response demonstrates **comprehension** by providing a **mostly accurate** explanation/description/comparison and by referencing the text(s) explicitly.
Score Point 1	The student response demonstrates **limited comprehension** and **may** reference the text(s) explicitly.
Score Point 0	The student response does not demonstrate comprehension of the text(s).

Construct Measured	
Writing **Written Expression**	
Score Point 3	The student response: • addresses the prompt and provides **effective** development of the topic that is **consistently appropriate** to the task by using **clear** reasoning and **relevant, text-based** evidence; • **consistently** demonstrates **purposeful and controlled** organization; • uses language to express ideas with clarity.
Score Point 2	The student response: • addresses the prompt and provides **some** development of the topic that is **generally appropriate** to the task by using reasoning and **relevant, text-based** evidence; • **generally** demonstrates **purposeful and controlled** organization; • uses language to express ideas with **some** clarity.

Score Point 1	The student response: • addresses the prompt and provides **minimal** development of the topic that is **limited in its appropriateness** to the task by using **limited** reasoning and **text-based** evidence; or • is a developed, text-based response with **little or no awareness** of the prompt; • demonstrates **purposeful** organization that **sometimes is not controlled**; • uses language to express ideas with limited clarity.
Score Point 0	The student response: • is **undeveloped** and/or **inappropriate** to the task; • demonstrates **little or no** organization; • does not use language to express ideas with clarity.

Construct Measured Writing Knowledge of Language and Conventions	
Score Point 3	The student response to the prompt demonstrates **full command** of the conventions of standard English at an appropriate level of complexity. There **may** be a **few minor errors** in mechanics, grammar, and usage, but **meaning is clear**.
Score Point 2	The student response to the prompt demonstrates **some command** of the conventions of standard English at an appropriate level of complexity. There **may** be errors in mechanics, grammar, and usage that **occasionally impede understanding**, but the **meaning is generally clear**.
Score Point 1	The student response to the prompt demonstrates **limited command** of the conventions of standard English at an appropriate level of complexity. There **may** be errors in mechanics, grammar, and usage that **often impede understanding**.
Score Point 0	The student response to the prompt demonstrates **no command** of the conventions of standard English. **Frequent and varied errors** in mechanics, grammar, and usage **impede understanding**.

APPENDIX B

Grade 3 Common Core Standards

The following standards offer a focus for instruction each year and help ensure that students gain adequate exposure to a range of texts and tasks. Rigor is also infused through the requirement that students read increasingly complex texts through the grades. Students advancing through the grades are expected to meet each year's grade-specific standards and retain or further develop skills and understandings mastered in preceding grades.

Reading Standards for Literature (RL)
Key Ideas and Details
Standard (RL.3.1): Ask and answer questions to demonstrate understanding of a text, referring explicitly to the text as the basis for the answers.
Standard (RL.3.2): Recount stories, including fables, folktales, and myths from diverse cultures; determine the central message, lesson, or moral and explain how it is conveyed through key details in the text.
Standard (RL.3.3): Describe characters in a story (e.g., their traits, motivations, or feelings) and explain how their actions contribute to the sequence of events.
Craft and Structure
Standard (RL.3.4): Determine the meaning of words and phrases as they are used in a text, distinguishing literal from nonliteral language.
Standard (RL.3.5): Refer to parts of stories, dramas, and poems when writing or speaking about a text, using terms such as chapter, scene, and stanza; describe how each successive part builds on earlier sections.
Standard (RL.3.6): Distinguish their own point of view from that of the narrator or those of the characters.

Reading Standards for Literature (RL)
Integration of Knowledge and Ideas
Standard (RL.3.7): Explain how specific aspects of a text's illustrations contribute to what is conveyed by the words in a story (e.g., create mood, emphasize aspects of a character or setting).
Standard (RL.3.8): (Not applicable to literature)
Standard (RL.3.9): Compare and contrast the themes, settings, and plots of stories written by the same author about the same or similar characters (e.g., in books from a series).
Range of Reading and Level of Text Complexity
Standard (RL.3.10): By the end of the year, read and comprehend literature, including stories, dramas, and poetry, at the high end of the grades 2–3 text complexity band independently and proficiently.

Reading Standards for Informational Text (RI)
Key Ideas and Details
Standard (RI.3.1): Ask and answer questions to demonstrate understanding of a text, referring explicitly to the text as the basis for the answers.
Standard (RI.3.2): Determine the main idea of a text: recount the key details and explain how they support the main idea.
Standard (RI.3.3): Describe the relationship between a series of historical events, scientific ideas or concepts, or steps in technical procedures in a text, using language that pertains to time, sequence, and cause/effect.
Craft and Structure
Standard (RI.3.4): Determine the meaning of general academic and domain-specific words and phrases in a text relevant to a grade 3 topic or subject area.
Standard (RI.3.5): Use text features and search tools (e.g., key words, sidebars, hyperlinks) to locate information relevant to a given topic efficiently.
Standard (RI.3.6): Distinguish their own point of view from that of the author of a text.

Reading Standards for Informational Text (RI)
Integration of Knowledge and Ideas
Standard (RI.3.7): Use information gained from illustrations (e.g., maps, photographs) and the words in a text to demonstrate understanding of the text (e.g., where, when, why, and how key events occur).
Standard (RI.3.8): Describe the logical connection between particular sentences and paragraphs in a text (e.g., comparison, cause/effect, first/second/third in a sequence).
Standard (RI.3.9): Compare and contrast the most important points and key details presented in two texts on the same topic.
Range of Reading and Level of Text Complexity
Standard (RI.3.10): By the end of the year, read and comprehend informational texts, including history/social studies, science, and technical texts, at the high end of the grades 2–3 text complexity band independently and proficiently.

Reading Standards: Foundational Skills (RF)
The standards are directed toward fostering students' understanding and working knowledge of concepts of print, the alphabetic principle, and other basic conventions of the English writing system. These foundational skills are not an end in and of themselves; rather, they are necessary and important components of an effective, comprehensive reading program designed to develop proficient readers with the capacity to comprehend texts across a range of types and disciplines. Instruction should be differentiated: good readers will need much less practice with these concepts than struggling readers will. The point is to teach students what they need to learn and not what they already know—to discern when particular children or activities warrant more or less attention.

Reading Standards: Foundational Skills (RF)

Phonics and Word Recognition

Standard (RF.3.3): Know and apply grade-level phonics and word analysis skills in decoding words.

Standard (RF.3.3a): Identify and know the meaning of the most common prefixes and derivational suffixes.

Standard (RF.3.3b): Decode words with common Latin suffixes.

Standard (RF.3.3c): Decode multisyllable words.

Standard (RF.3.3d): Read grade-appropriate irregularly spelled words.

Fluency

Standard (RF.3.4): Read with sufficient accuracy and fluency to support comprehension.

Standard (RF.3.4a): Read on-level text with purpose and understanding.

Standard (RF.3.4b): Read on-level prose and poetry orally with accuracy, appropriate rate, and expression on successive readings.

Standard (RF.3.4c): Use context to confirm or self-correct word recognition and understanding, rereading as necessary.

Writing Standards (W)

The following standards for K–5 offer a focus for instruction each year to help ensure that students gain adequate mastery of a range of skills and applications. Each year in their writing, students should demonstrate increasing sophistication in all aspects of language use, from vocabulary and syntax to the development and organization of ideas, and they should address increasingly demanding content and sources. Students advancing through the grades are expected to meet each year's grade-specific standards and retain or further develop skills and understandings mastered in preceding grades. The expected growth in student writing ability is reflected both in the standards themselves and in the collection of annotated student writing samples in Appendix C.

Writing Standards (W)
Text Types and Purposes
Standard (W.3.1): Write opinion pieces on topics or texts, supporting a point of view with reasons. **Standard (W.3.1a):** Introduce the topic or text they are writing about, state an opinion, and create an organizational structure that lists reasons. **Standard (W.3.1b):** Provide reasons that support the opinion. **Standard (W.3.1c):** Use linking words and phrases (e.g., because, therefore, since, for example) to connect opinion and reasons. **Standard (W.3.1d):** Provide a concluding statement or section.
Standard (W.3.2): Write informative/explanatory texts to examine a topic and convey ideas and information clearly. **Standard (W.3.2a):** Introduce a topic and group related information together; include illustrations when useful to aiding comprehension. **Standard (W.3.2b):** Develop the topic with facts, definitions, and details. **Standard (W.3.2c):** Use linking words and phrases (e.g., also, another, and, more, but) to connect ideas within categories of information. **Standard (W.3.2d):** Provide a concluding statement or section.
Standard (W.3.3): Write narratives to develop real or imagined experiences or events using effective technique, descriptive details, and clear event sequences. **Standard (W.3.3a):** Establish a situation and introduce a narrator and/or characters; organize an event sequence that unfolds naturally. **Standard (W.3.3b):** Use dialogue and descriptions of actions, thoughts, and feelings to develop experiences and events or show the response of characters to situations. **Standard (W.3.3c):** Use temporal words and phrases to signal event order. **Standard (W.3.3d):** Provide a sense of closure.

Writing Standards (W)
Production and Distribution of Writing
Standard (W.3.4): With guidance and support from adults, produce writing in which the development and organization are appropriate to task and purpose. (Grade-specific expectations for writing types are defined in standards 1–3 above.)
Standard (W.3.5): With guidance and support from peers and adults, develop and strengthen writing as needed by planning, revising, and editing. (Editing for conventions should demonstrate command of Language standards 1–3 up to and including grade 3.)
Standard (W.3.6): With guidance and support from adults, use technology to produce and publish writing (using keyboarding skills) as well as to interact and collaborate with others.
Research to Build and Present Knowledge
Standard (W.3.7): Conduct short research projects that build knowledge about a topic.
Standard (W.3.8): Recall information from experiences or gather information from print and digital sources; take brief notes on sources and sort evidence into provided categories.
Standard (W.3.9): (Begins in grade 4)
Range of Writing
Standard (W.3.10): Write routinely over extended time frames (time for research, reflection, and revision) and shorter time frames (a single sitting or a day or two) for a range of discipline-specific tasks, purposes, and audiences.

Speaking and Listening Standards (SL)
The following standards for K–5 offer a focus for instruction each year to help ensure that students gain adequate mastery of a range of skills and applications. Students advancing through the grades are expected to meet each year's grade-specific standards and retain or further develop skills and understandings mastered in preceding grades.

Speaking and Listening Standards (SL)
Comprehension and Collaboration
Standard (SL.3.1): Engage effectively in a range of collaborative discussions (one-on-one, in groups, and teacher-led) with diverse partners on grade 3 topics and texts, building on others' ideas and expressing their own clearly. **Standard (SL.3.1a):** Come to discussions prepared, having read or studied required material; explicitly draw on that preparation and other information known about the topic to explore ideas under discussion. **Standard (SL.3.1b):** Follow agreed-upon rules for discussions (e.g., gaining the floor in respectful ways, listening to others with care, speaking one at a time about the topics and texts under discussion). **Standard (SL.3.1c):** Ask questions to check understanding of information presented, stay on topic, and link their comments to the remarks of others. **Standard (SL.3.1d):** Explain their own ideas and understanding in light of the discussion.
Standard (SL.3.2): Determine the main ideas and supporting details of a text read aloud or information presented in diverse media and formats, including visually, quantitatively, and orally.
Standard (SL.3.3): Ask and answer questions about information from a speaker, offering appropriate elaboration and detail.
Presentation of Knowledge and Ideas
Standard (SL.3.4): Report on a topic or text, tell a story, or recount an experience with appropriate facts and relevant, descriptive details, speaking clearly at an understandable pace.
Standard (SL.3.5): Create engaging audio recordings of stories or poems that demonstrate fluid reading at an understandable pace; add visual displays when appropriate to emphasize or enhance certain facts or details.
Standard (SL.3.6): Speak in complete sentences when appropriate to task and situation in order to provide requested detail or clarification. (See grade 3 Language standards 1 and 3 for specific expectations.)

Language Standards (L)

The following standards for K-5 offer a focus for instruction each year to help ensure that students gain adequate mastery of a range of skills and applications. Students advancing through the grades are expected to meet each year's grade-specific standards and retain or further develop skills and understandings mastered in preceding grades. Beginning in grade 3, skills and understandings that are particularly likely to require continued attention in higher grades as they are applied to increasingly sophisticated writing and speaking are marked with an asterisk (*). See the table on page 30 for a complete list and Appendix A for an example of how these skills develop in sophistication.

Conventions of Standard English

Standard (L.3.1): Demonstrate command of the conventions of standard English grammar and usage when writing or speaking.

Standard (L.3.1a): Explain the function of nouns, pronouns, verbs, adjectives, and adverbs in general and their functions in particular sentences.

Standard (L.3.1b): Form and use regular and irregular plural nouns.

Standard (L.3.1c): Use abstract nouns (e.g., childhood).

Standard (L.3.1d): Form and use regular and irregular verbs.

Standard (L.3.1e): Form and use the simple (e.g., I walked; I walk; I will walk) verb tenses.

Standard (L.3.1f): Ensure subject-verb and pronoun-antecedent agreement.*

Standard (L.3.1g): Form and use comparative and superlative adjectives and adverbs, and choose between them depending on what is to be modified.

Standard (L.3.1h): Use coordinating and subordinating conjunctions.

Standard (L.3.1i): Produce simple, compound, and complex sentences.

Language Standards (L)

Standard (L.3.2): Demonstrate command of the conventions of standard English capitalization, punctuation, and spelling when writing.

Standard (L.3.2a): Capitalize appropriate words in titles.

Standard (L.3.2b): Use commas in addresses.

Standard (L.3.2c): Use commas and quotation marks in dialogue.

Standard (L.3.2d): Form and use possessives.

Standard (L.3.2e): Use conventional spelling for high-frequency and other studied words and for adding suffixes to base words (e.g., sitting, smiled, cries, happiness).

Standard (L.3.2f): Use spelling patterns and generalizations (e.g., word families, position-based spellings, syllable patterns, ending rules, meaningful word parts) in writing words.

Standard (L.3.2g): Consult reference materials, including beginning dictionaries, as needed to check and correct spellings.

Standard (L.3.3): Use knowledge of language and its conventions when writing, speaking, reading, or listening.

Standard (L.3.3a): Choose words and phrases for effect.*

Standard (L.3.3b): Recognize and observe differences between the conventions of spoken and written standard English.

Vocabulary Acquisition and Use

Standard (L.3.4): Determine or clarify the meaning of unknown and multiple-meaning words and phrases based on grade 3 reading and content, choosing flexibly from a range of strategies.

Standard (L.3.4a): Use sentence-level context as a clue to the meaning of a word or phrase.

Standard (L.3.4b): Determine the meaning of the new word formed when a known affix is added to a known word (e.g., agreeable/disagreeable, comfortable/uncomfortable, care/careless, heat/preheat).

Standard (L.3.4c): Use a known root word as a clue to the meaning of an unknown word with the same root (e.g., company, companion).

Standard (L.3.4d): Use glossaries or beginning dictionaries, both print and digital, to determine or clarify the precise meaning of key words and phrases.

Language Standards (L)
Standard (L.3.5): Demonstrate understanding of word relationships and nuances in word meanings. **Standard (L.3.5a):** Distinguish the literal and nonliteral meanings of words and phrases in context (e.g., take steps). **Standard (L.3.5b):** Identify real-life connections between words and their use (e.g., describe people who are friendly or helpful). **Standard (L.3.5c):** Distinguish shades of meaning among related words that describe states of mind or degrees of certainty (e.g., knew, believed, suspected, heard, wondered).
Standard (L.3.6): Acquire and use accurately grade-appropriate conversational, general academic, and domain-specific words and phrases, including those that signal spatial and temporal relationships (e.g., After dinner that night we went looking for them).

Index